Happily Ever After

Happily Ever After

A REAL-LIFE LOOK AT YOUR
FIRST YEAR OF MARRIAGE

TOBEN AND JOANNE HEIM

NAVPRESS ®

BRINGING TRUTH TO LIFE

The Navigators is an international Christian organization. Our mission is to reach, disciple, and equip people to know Christ and to make Him known through successive generations. We envision multitudes of diverse people in the United States and every other nation who have a passionate love for Christ, live a lifestyle of sharing Christ's love, and multiply spiritual laborers among those without Christ.

NavPress is the publishing ministry of The Navigators. NavPress publications help believers learn biblical truth and apply what they learn to their lives and ministries. Our mission is to stimulate spiritual formation among our readers.

© 2000, 2004 by Toben and Joanne Heim

Previously published as *Great Expectations*.

All rights reserved. No part of this publication may be reproduced in any form without written permission from NavPress, P.O. Box 35001, Colorado Springs, CO 80935. www.navpress.com

NAVPRESS, BRINGING TRUTH TO LIFE, and the NAVPRESS logo are registered trademarks of NavPress. Absence of ® in connection with marks of NavPress or other parties does not indicate an absence of registration of those marks.

ISBN 1-57683-528-6

Cover design by Chris Gilbert, UDG | DesignWorks
Cover photo by Photodisc
Creative Team: Greg Clouse, Kathy Mosier, Glynese Northam

Some of the anecdotal illustrations in this book are true to life and are included with the permission of the persons involved. All other illustrations are composites of real situations, and any resemblance to people living or dead is coincidental.

Unless otherwise identified, all Scripture quotations in this publication are taken from THE MESSAGE (MSG). Copyright © 1993, 1994, 1995, 1996, 2000, 2001, 2002. Used by permission of NavPress Publishing Group. Other versions used include the HOLY BIBLE: NEW INTERNATIONAL VERSION® (NIV®). Copyright © 1973, 1978, 1984 by International Bible Society. Used by permission of Zondervan Publishing House. All rights reserved; the *New American Standard Bible* (NASB), © The Lockman Foundation 1960, 1962, 1963, 1968, 1971, 1972, 1973, 1975, 1977; and the King James Version (KJV).

Heim, Toben, 1970-
  Happily ever after : a real-life look at your first year of marriage /
Toben and Joanne Heim.
    p. cm.
Rev. ed. of: Great expectations.
Includes bibliographical references (p.   ).
  ISBN 1-57683-528-6
  1. Married people. 2. Marriage. 3. Married people--Religious life.
4. Marriage--Religious aspects--Christianity. I. Heim, Joanne, 1972-
II. Heim, Toben, 1970- Great expectations. III. Title.
  HQ734.H4723 2003
  306.81--dc22

                    2003019342

Printed in Canada
1 2 3 4 5 6 7 8 9 10 / 08 07 06 05 04

FOR A FREE CATALOG OF NAVPRESS BOOKS & BIBLE STUDIES,
CALL 1-800-366-7788 (USA) OR 1-416-499-4615 (CANADA)

To Charles and Kay Friedenstein, you have shown us what it means to have a godly marriage. We appreciate your example and knowing you're always there for us. We love you.

And to our dear friends,
Brian and Hanna.
We wish you every joy in your life together.

This is my lover, this my friend.

— Song of Songs 5:16, NIV

Table of Contents

Acknowledgments

Thanks to Mom, Susan, and Colleen for the babysitting you did to help us get this written without stopping to change diapers.

Thanks to all of our friends at NavPress who encouraged us along the way and showed their excitement to publish this book. And thanks to Brad Lewis for all of his editorial help.

Thanks to Chris Palmer at Air Academy High School, the best English teacher we both had, for teaching us to write a composition.

Thanks to all of the people who were willing to talk to us about their marriages — especially Robb and Rebecca, Brad and Kim, Brian and Hanna, Dave and Kathy, Doug and Lisa, Larry and Kathy, Kevin and Mary, Gordon and Sue, Rich and Kim, Kathy and Bob, Jan and Bob, and Steve and Darlene.

Preface

To the New Edition

It's hard to believe that it's been five years since we came up with the idea for this book. So much has changed in many ways. Our "new" baby just turned five, and her little sister is almost three! After living in Colorado for the past ten years, we're now in the middle of a move to Southern California. New job, new house, new schools, new everything!

At the same time, so many things haven't really changed. We still struggle with money issues. (Working out a new budget while taking into account a much higher cost of living has proved that!) We still need to put stress aside and have fun in order to keep balance during crazy and hectic times. And we still rely on the community of friends we have found to support us when the going gets tough.

While we wrote this book for couples just starting out, reading it again over the past few weeks to prepare for this new edition reminded me how important it is to take the time to think about the building blocks of marriage as the years go by. Good communication is always important and can always be improved — whether you've been married for twelve months or twelve years. The same goes for working out constructive ways to deal with conflict, keeping sex new and exciting, and finding new and creative ways to celebrate together.

We hope you enjoy reading *Happily Ever After* and wish you a lifetime of joy together!

Toben and Joanne Heim

SEPTEMBER 2003

What to Expect When You Say "I Do"

JOANNE:

I could hardly wait to get married. Toben and I were engaged the night before I graduated from high school (yes, my parents have recovered!) and knew we'd have a long engagement. We wanted a winter wedding and needed more than six months to get ready. That meant being engaged for a year and a half.

With eighteen months of dreaming and planning, I had plenty of time to build up my expectations for marriage. I would magically become as beautiful as I'd always dreamed of being, instantly know how to cook gourmet meals (when we got engaged I could make toast and macaroni and cheese — from a box), and leave all my problems behind. To make everything perfect, we would never, ever fight.

I know it sounds silly, but I really thought marriage would turn me into a new and improved version of me. Unrealistic? Definitely. But did that make me stop to think that I was setting myself up for some big disappointments? Not really.

The wedding went off without a hitch. Our plans came together perfectly, and I assumed that our marriage would come off equally well.

Never mind that we made a lot of wedding plans but not very many marriage plans.

Looking back, the first month of marriage was one of ups and downs. January at Whitworth College was its own term, and we didn't take classes. We slept in, worked a little, and settled into our new life together. I enjoyed setting the table each night with new dishes, new candlesticks, new linens, and a new experiment in cooking. I wrote endless thank-you notes while watching *Days of Our Lives* and the falling snow outside.

Still, being married wasn't quite what I had expected. Toben didn't bring me breakfast in bed. Sex wasn't nearly the rapturous experience that Harlequin romances led me to believe. We didn't have long prayer times or daily devotions together. We fought about stupid things (how to arrange the towels in the linen closet) as if they were life-and-death matters. And all of my same insecurities followed me wherever I went.

The thing I didn't like about being married was that being married didn't make me happy like I expected it would. And Toben couldn't always make me feel happy like I expected him to. So what went wrong?

We had gone to premarital counseling. We had read all the "right" books — on marriage, sex, communication, finances, and a host of other things. We wanted to have the best marriage ever. So why wasn't it all working according to plan?

*T*OBEN:

My expectations were much less defined than Joanne's. But I also expected to become a better version of myself — Toben 2.0. I expected to become a responsible adult, a man who put away childish things and set about the serious business of being a husband. I expected to be

14

mature, thoughtful, intelligent, and everything Joanne could ever dream of in a mate. And I would become all of that overnight. It was a tall order for a twenty-one-year-old, but I was convinced I could be that guy.

I knew that I loved Joanne more than anything in the world (almost from the moment we met!) and that I wanted to be with her for the rest of my life. I thought we were in for complete postnuptial bliss. Within hours of our wedding, my assumptions were challenged. Within a month, my assumptions were *gone*.

Let's start at the beginning. Our wedding was beautiful and the reception was wonderful — and *long*. When we finally escaped, it was close to midnight, and we were pelted with enough birdseed to choke Big Bird. The hotel that we had decided on for our first night as a married couple was half an hour away — just far enough for us to fall asleep in the back of the limousine.

By the time we got to our room we were groggy and deeply in need of food, sleep, and a shower. And if we'd left it at that, it would have been best. But everyone knows that a newly married couple is supposed to have sex on their wedding night. Neither of us was particularly experienced but we gave it a go — to less-than-anticipated results.

On to Carmel the next day for the remainder of our honeymoon. We had a blast, except that Joanne battled a flu bug for part of the time and we racked up a credit card debt that took years to pay off.

Back to college and "real" life. The honeymoon was over. And a few days later, when we got into our first post-married fight about how the towels should be folded, I knew things weren't going to be as easy as I'd imagined. That's when the real work of being married began for me.

As a guy, I might not have felt the same emotional distress that Joanne experienced during those early days. But I do remember the high-highs and low-lows that accompanied this time in our lives, and the beginnings of a process that we continue to this day — a process of coming together as two people who love each other very much and who occasionally drive each other completely crazy.

The last thing I'd want you to think is that I have negative memories of our first year together. I wouldn't change a thing. I wouldn't change our first too-small apartment and our adventures in Ramen noodle preparation. I wouldn't miss our day trips to the lake during a mercilessly hot summer or the blizzard that buried our car under three feet of snow. I wouldn't trade the late nights of homework, student government meetings, and eleventh-hour work on the college newspaper that pushed us to our emotional limits. And I wouldn't give up the warm feeling I got when I realized that no matter where we ended up during the day, we would end up together at night. But most of all, I wouldn't trade those first uncertain steps we made on weak, baby legs that led us to rely on each other, on our families, and on God.

KNOCKING OFF CORNERS

*J*OANNE:

One of my best friends from high school got married last summer. At one point she asked me what being married was like. "It's wonderful!" I said. "Except when it's not."

Toben says that when we get married, we're each like a square paving stone. The goal of marriage is to make us smooth, round paving stones. The first year knocks off our corners, leaving ragged edges and raw scars. As each year passes, it smooths out those edges as we become more of who we're meant to be.

*T*OBEN:

Let me expand a little. Every one of us comes into marriage with a set of behaviors, preferences, opinions, habits, and "a way of doing things." The person you marry has his or her own list of distinctives.

Say, for example, that you always put the toilet paper on the roller so that the paper comes over the top and your spouse is used to putting it on so that it comes off the bottom. The first time you see it "the wrong way" you will either change it to the way you like it or live with it. If you're like me and you decide to change it, you'll probably have to say something to go along with your change. "Honey," you casually say when you exit the bathroom, "I put the toilet paper on the roller the *right* way. Don't you know that it's supposed to come over the top?"

Your spouse may or may not react well to this suggestion. But because toilet paper is relatively minor in the grand scheme of things, it probably won't end too badly when it's all said and done. Chip. Off comes a little edge of corner as the two of you negotiate the finer points of toilet paper. Not too painful.

But say you decide to go golfing with your friends one Saturday morning. You kiss your bride goodbye and head to the course. You hit some range balls, practice your putting, play eighteen holes, grab a Coke afterward, and end up back at your house seven hours later to find your spouse ready to kill you. "I thought you said it took four hours to play a round of golf. You were gone for seven!" she says through clenched teeth.

17

Maybe your parents came and went as they pleased, breezing in and out of the house. But maybe her parents kept each other informed of their daily activities down to the minutest detail. So when you came home late, it was a shock to her expectations and her way of doing things.

Chip, chip, chip. Chances are, as you work through this one, big chunks of your corners (and hers) will be knocked off as you begin to establish your own patterns for doing things.

*J*OANNE:

Our first year of marriage wasn't what I expected. I had a lot of corners to be knocked off — things like wanting my own way and putting my needs and desires before Toben's. But as each year has passed, the smoothing process has become a little easier as we've learned to care for each other and put the other ahead of ourselves.

We think being married is a lot of fun, and we want to help you build a solid foundation in your first year that will last a lifetime. That's why we've written *Happily Ever After: A Real-Life Look at Your First Year of Marriage.* It's designed to help you prepare for the first year by examining your expectations and helping you understand them and communicate them to your partner.

HOW THIS BOOK WORKS

Happily Ever After is divided into eight chapters — each one dealing with an area of marriage that can be a source of unmet expectations during the first year. We realize, of course, that each marriage is different and not everyone will struggle with the same issues. Our goal was to pick

18

topics that most couples can relate to. We also understand that men and women often view issues differently — and therefore deal with them differently. For this reason, *Happily Ever After* is written from both a husband's and a wife's perspectives.

In each chapter of this book, you will find a number of common elements:

The "First Steps" of newlyweds. We asked some newly married friends of ours, Brian and Hanna, to answer some questions to give you an idea of what they think about marriage just a few months into it. You'll find their interchanges throughout the chapters.

The "Voice of Wisdom" from couples who are older and wiser. Advice from couples who've been married a long time is something that's often hard to find in a time when divorce is so common. Couples whose marriages have stood the test of time are rare. The "Voice of Wisdom" section offers advice and encouragement from those couples who have stuck together — through thick and thin.

Questions for couples to work through both individually and together. One of the ways to avoid unmet or unrealistic expectations is to talk about them. But it can be difficult to know where to start. These questions are designed to get you thinking and talking about your expectations for marriage. Sometimes it can be difficult to voice your expectations and feelings — even to your one and only. For many people, it's easier to express emotions on paper. That's why we've starred certain questions that are ideal for journaling. Consider purchasing a journal or spiral notebook to write down your thoughts and feelings. Then share your discoveries with your spouse.

A wide variety of excellent resources are available on the subject of marriage. At the end of this book you'll find resources and recommended reading to give you a more in-depth look at a particular issue, an opposing viewpoint, or a place to go for more answers. We've tried to include complete information for each of these books. Finding them is simple — check out Amazon.com. We recommend doing your own search for other books on the topic. As much as we love to read, there are just too many books out there and too little time for us to note all of them!

One other note: We're not marriage experts and don't have all the answers, but we have found benefits in asking questions. Remember that this book is for engaged and newly married couples. We're not trying to fix long-standing problems, but rather we want to identify some common issues in order to give you a head start in avoiding them. Our hope is that by reading this book and answering some of the questions in it, you'll learn about both yourself and your spouse and see the ways that God has created you to be partners in marriage. The best place to start learning these things is at the beginning — where you come from.

CHAPTER ONE

Where You Come From

FAMILY HISTORY

JOANNE:

"I, Joanne, take you, Toben, to be my lawfully wedded husband . . . and your mother to be my mother-in-law . . . and your father to be my father-in-law . . . and your sister to be my sister-in-law . . . and your. . . ."

Let's face it — you're marrying more than just your spouse. In a sense, you're marrying your spouse's family too. So it's important to take a good look at where you each come from and the family history that shapes who you are as individuals.

"But we're not living anywhere near either of our families," you say. "This isn't a big deal for us." We beg to differ. In fact, we think that where you come from and your family history lies beneath just about every issue you'll face in your entire marriage — not just in the first year.

We have a theory that when the going gets tough, your first instinct is to go with what was modeled to you — no matter how tough you are. Going with what was modeled isn't necessarily bad, but chances are that what was modeled to you was different from what was modeled to your spouse. And if you grew up in any sort of normal family, there is at least a little bit of dysfunction that may pop up in your marriage when things get rough.

This isn't the only reason to take a good look at each other's family. Where did you learn about marriage? From your parents. Our parents shape our views about marriage. They teach us what it looks like to manage money, to make decisions, and to raise children in partnership with another person. Where you come from is something worth looking at when it comes to marriage.

And remember, you are still a part of your family even though you're married. Learn to listen when your spouse has input about your parents and your family, even though it can be hard. Talk about how you as a couple want to relate with your families.

MEET OUR FAMILIES

On the surface, our families seemed to be pretty similar. Both families were living in Los Angeles when we were born. Both families had two kids and an assortment of dogs. Both families moved to Colorado Springs in the late 1970s. Both families sent their kids to Christian schools (same town, different schools). Both families were actively involved in their churches. Both families later moved to the same neighborhood — a few blocks apart. Both sets of parents are still married to each other.

But if you dig a little deeper, you'll see some big differences in the way our families operate that caused us some trouble early in our marriage. Take disagreements, for example. In Toben's family, you debate to win your point and draw on all available resources to do so. So when Toben was about five years old and decided he needed cap guns to be a happy, well-rounded child, he gave a persuasive speech, debated the opposing evidence, and ended up with the guns. On the other hand, as a child in my family, all opinions were valid, but Mom and Dad had the final say. So when I decided that I just had to have a Barbie townhouse complete with elevator, Mom and Dad said no, and that was the end of it.

What do cap guns and Barbie houses have to do with being married? A lot. In early disagreements, Toben came on like a steamroller. I felt bombarded by the argument and cut to the quick if I disagreed. I was stunned into silence — which Toben often took as compliance — only to find out an hour, a day, or a year later that I wasn't completely on board with whatever the plan was. Talk about expectations going unmet! Toben expected me to debate with the same intensity he did, and I expected a conversation rather than a speech.

Luckily, we've learned how our families and our personalities affect our disagreements, and now we're actually pretty good when it comes to dealing with opposing viewpoints. (We'll talk more about that in a later chapter.)

Once we took the time to learn how our families were different in spite of all the similarities, things got easier. That's not to say that all of the pieces just fell into place one day. But by understanding where we came from and what was modeled, we have a better chance of ending up on the same page when it is all said and done.

The same thing applies to how we spend money, celebrate holidays, view worship and church, and do just about everything else in our marriage. We can't say it enough: Where you come from plays a huge

23

role in your marriage. Without taking the time to learn about each other's family, you're headed for trouble.

BOUND TO REPEAT IT

*T*OBEN:

In a lot of ways I'm like my father. I have his mannerisms. I make the same strange noises he does to punctuate my speech. I spend money like he does. We share a love for toys (pens, pocket knives, watches, and anything gadgety). We are both faithful to a fault but quick to change if we feel like we've been betrayed. I can learn a lot about myself by reflecting on who he is. Chances are, if he is a particular way, I am too. Some things about him I want to emulate, but a few things I want to change in myself. He has a great sense of humor, and he works hard and really throws himself into the things he does. Mom used to say that when Dad decided to do something, he'd read a book about it and then just do it. I hope at least some of that is in me. All of Dad's behaviors have been modeled to me — I've seen them in context and they come naturally to me — so continuing with the good behaviors is relatively easy.

But emulating those good things is often easier than changing the things I want to change. Knowing what you don't want to be is easy. Not being it isn't. Knowing Joanne's family history has been a great help because Joanne's dad effectively models some of the ways I want to be. I have a tendency to be foolish with my money but Joanne's dad is great with money. I have learned — and continue to learn — a lot from him.

I think the same is true for Joanne and my mom. My mom has empowered Joanne in some ways to be who she wants to be. She has

24

modeled a strength and force of conviction that I see glimpses of in Joanne from time to time. One of the truly great things about getting married is the chance to adopt another history that weaves together with your own to create a fabric that is similar to the one your parents wove, but is also unique to your new family of two.

THE STORY BEHIND THE STORY

When I was a kid I could be very cruel. I made fun of people who were overweight, unattractive, or anything else I didn't like. One summer when I was living with my aunt and uncle in California, I was ranting, carrying on, and generally being mean. My uncle stopped me and said, "Behind every story, there is a story. People are the way they are for a reason. Until you know that story, shut up!"

In retrospect, and knowing my uncle as well as I do, I don't think he actually told me to shut up. But his meaning was clear and continues to ring in my ears some twenty years later. If someone does something that doesn't make sense to me, I should take the opportunity to discover his or her story. This may help me understand whatever it is that doesn't make sense to me.

Never has this principle been more important to me than in my marriage. Joanne does stuff from time to time that seems absolutely loony to me, though it happens less frequently now than in the beginning.

When we were first married, we would disagree about something and Joanne would withdraw more and more into herself. In my family we went toe-to-toe, so when Joanne shut down, it drove me nuts.

Turns out, that's the way things were in her family. They didn't have a lot of conflict, but when they did, Joanne's dad would lay down the law and that was that. The subject was not open for discussion. It was natural for Joanne to withdraw when conflict would arise, but it was terribly unnatural for me. Understanding her story helped me make sense of that behavior. For Joanne, understanding my story helped her understand why I would get more and more upset when she withdrew.

We learned this lesson and many others the hard way. One way or another, you'll discover all kinds of things about each other that stem from your past, your story. The more opportunity you have to share those stories with one another, the less you'll learn the hard way.

26

UH, WHAT PAGE ARE YOU ON?

*J*OANNE:

In their book *Marriage Takes More Than Love,* Jack and Carole Mayhall describe couples who have different family backgrounds as having different scripts to the same play. You and your spouse begin the scene, only to find out you're on totally different pages of two different scripts.

Imagine this scene: It's Sunday afternoon and you've just come home from church. You've planned a big Sunday dinner like you always had growing up. The next thing you know, your husband has not only changed out of his church clothes, he's outside mowing the lawn! Doesn't he know that Sunday afternoons start with Sunday dinner, followed by a leisurely walk and a nap? What does he think he's doing?!

We said before that when you get married, you marry more than your spouse. You marry your spouse's family too. More specifically, you marry your partner's script of what marriage and family look like. So how does this play out in everyday life?

What were mornings like in your family? If you ate breakfast together each morning before heading off to work and school, chances are that's what you envisioned for your own future. But what if the love of your life's family skipped breakfast altogether and barely had time to say good morning before rushing out the door?

What about dinner? Was dinner in your family a sit-down, home-cooked affair when each person shared about his or her day and plans for the next? Or was dinner whatever you could find, eaten in front of the television?

For our friends Brian and Hanna, dinner is something their families had completely different scripts for. "In my family," says Hanna, "dinner was not an option. My mom cooked every night, and we were all expected to be there. We ate in the dining room and would sit at the table for over two hours each night. We'd talk about what we did that day, what was coming up tomorrow, or anything else on our minds. It was an important part of our day."

"My family was totally different," says Brian. "We ate out a lot, and there wasn't really any expectation to be there. When we did eat at home, we ate in the kitchen with the television on."

So how have they defined dinner for themselves as a married couple? "I really like how Hanna's family did dinner," Brian says. "We value conversation and don't even have a television in our apartment."

Still, it isn't easy to switch scripts. "There are still days when I want to jump up and clear the table as soon as we're done eating," he says. "I forget how nice it is to sit and talk."

What was church like for you? In my family, church was not an option. We were there each Sunday, rain or shine. And if one of us was sick, he or she stayed home and watched church on television. For Toben's family, church was important, but negotiable. For them, a Sunday morning might just as easily have meant a drive in the mountains or a leisurely brunch as a family.

Who did the laundry? Who put gas in the cars? Who cooked? Who cleaned up? Who drove? It may seem trivial, but these kinds of little things are the things that shape our expectations of marriage.

Toben's dad, Lowell, often cleaned up the dishes after dinner. I guess he figured that since Pamela went to the trouble to make a nice meal, the least he could do was clean up and give her a break. So ever since Toben and I married, Toben cleans up after dinner too. In my family, my mom cooked and usually cleaned up afterward — until Kristen and I were old enough to do the dishes. I'm pretty sure that if Lowell hadn't modeled cleaning up the dinner dishes to Toben, I'd be doing both because that's all either one of us would have known.

LEAVE AND CLEAVE: THE IMPORTANCE OF BOUNDARIES

At one time, we lived five doors down from Toben's family. And we lived in a townhouse, so five doors down was the equivalent of about one hundred feet. My parents were just a twenty-minute drive away, and Toben's aunt and uncle lived only five minutes from us. Needless to say, we were completely surrounded.

So we're not quite like Adam and Eve. As the first couple ever, they weren't exactly typical. They knew they were right for each other from the start. Besides the fact that God quite literally made them for each other, there wasn't any other competition. As far as I can tell, they never planned a wedding. This eliminated a lot of potential disagreements like who to include in the wedding party, where to have the reception, what kind of food to serve, and who to invite — or not to invite. As the only people on earth, they didn't suffer from the trap of comparing each other to the man or woman across the street, in the cubicle next door, or sitting next to them at the traffic light. And let's face it — they didn't have in-laws.

Let me say right here that I have great parents-in-law. Toben's parents have loved me from the time Toben and I started dating and have shown that love to me in countless ways. They invited me on family trips, included me in family traditions, and told me a lot how much they loved me. In fact, Pamela never refers to me as her daughter-in-law, but always introduces me as her daughter-in-love.

I was talking with a woman the other day who was amazed that I'm still sane after having lived so close to my mother-in-law. "I thought the other end of town was too close," she said of her husband's mother. But living so close to Toben's parents has been great for us. We respect each other's homes, free time, and the right to say no to a last-minute dinner invitation.

Back to Adam and Eve. I think it's interesting that even though they didn't have parents, God still included this verse in the very beginning of the Bible: "For this reason a man will leave his father and mother and be united to his wife, and they will become one flesh" (Genesis 2:24, NIV).

One of the reasons this verse stands out to us is that you have to know what you're leaving in order to leave — especially when there's no great distance involved. It's all about family history. That's not to say that we're not supposed to do anything like our parents did, but as we've said before, it's important to look at where you came from and discuss that with your spouse.

So what does leaving and cleaving look like? In short, establishing clear boundaries. Many books have been written about boundaries, explaining what they are, why they're important, and how to set them with the people in your life — especially the difficult ones.

In a nutshell, boundaries are just what they sound like — lines (albeit invisible ones) that define how we operate. For example, because we lived so close to Toben's parents, it was easy to just drop by any time. And sometimes that was okay. But something we usually did out of respect for each other was call before stopping by. That way, we didn't interrupt dinner or family time — or catch them in their underwear!

Some boundaries — like calling before visiting — just happen naturally. Because my parents lived farther away, we called before going to their house. Other boundaries require more planning and more communication. *Not* talking about them is fertile ground for conflict. Whatever the issue, be realistic when setting boundaries. What may be a big deal to you may not be a big deal to your spouse.

FIRST STEPS

What boundaries have you set with your parents since getting married?
Hanna: We've not really set very many boundaries with my parents. They live in another state and have been intentional about giving

us our own space. They usually wait for us to call them and don't assume anything when it comes to where we'll spend the holidays.

Brian: My parents live in the same town as us. While we haven't set formal boundaries, we're learning to ask more and assume less.

THE DIVORCE EXPERIMENT

*T*OBEN:

While our views of marriage are shaped largely by our parents and our families, culture also plays an important role in how we perceive marriage. And one of the most dominant trends regarding marriage in our culture is divorce.

31

Culture influences us to such a degree that there may be nothing more powerful in the creation of our concept of marriage than divorce. This is true if your parents got divorced and may also be true if they are still together. Whether we like it or not, those of us who grew up in the seventies and eighties were part of "the divorce experiment." (I don't think I coined the term but I heard it somewhere and it stuck.)

It really did seem to be an experiment: "If our marriage isn't working out, we might as well try divorce. It can't be worse for the kids than seeing us argue all the time," parents reasoned. Some counselors even espoused this idea and suggested divorce as the best course of action, for the kids' sake.

Recently, quite a bit has been made of what a terrible fallacy all this was. The news comes a couple of decades too late for many of us who suffered through this lapse in judgment.

My parents are together, but I am still a product of the divorce experiment. Three of my best friends' parents divorced right around my freshman or sophomore year of high school. Adam's parents had "irreconcilable differences," Donner's dad had grown emotionally distant, and Holly's dad had an affair with her best friend's mom while the rest of the family was on vacation. Even though my parents told me they were together for the long haul, I always believed that divorce was an option for them. I thought that if the chips were down far enough, all bets were off.

I saw firsthand the effect divorce had on my friends. Each one suffered in unique and painful ways as the sins of their parents were revisited on them over and over again. I won't tell their stories here because they aren't mine to tell; suffice it to say, I was struck that if it could happen to them, maybe it could happen to me.

It wasn't much comfort that both my parents were Christians. Adam, Donner, and Holly were friends from my youth group. All of our parents went to the same church. Joanne and I went through the difficult experience of seeing a couple from our Sunday school class divorce after only a few years of marriage, as well as friends from our Christian college. Because statistics typically apply across the board, despite religious beliefs, Christian couples are probably as likely to divorce as nonChristian couples.

Even though I was affected by divorce, I can't fully comprehend the experience of having my own parents divorce, as those with divorced parents can. I was talking with my friend Kim today. She told me about the challenges she and her husband faced because his folks were divorced and hers were not. He carried around feelings of insecurity for years as a result, until they were able to talk about it and put those fears to rest.

As with everything in this book, all you can really do to get past fears and insecurities about divorce is talk — a lot. Put the fears, perceptions, insecurities, and expectations on the table and have at them. The wounds that divorce inflicts on everyone involved, especially the children of divorce, are not quickly or easily healed. Take your time to work through your feelings as a couple, but stay on purpose. It'll be worth the effort.

The only thing that will make our marriages different from the statistics is if we take our vows seriously and think about them all the time, especially when the chips are down. Don't allow yourself to think for even a second that anything else is an option.

THE NAME OF THE GAME IS CHANGE

*J*OANNE:

Let's face it — getting married involves a lot of changes. You have to change your driver's license, your bank accounts, your social security card, your address, your name, your signature, your magazine subscriptions, and a host of other things.

But even more than that changes. You change your lifestyle — and that's not very easy. Authors Larry and Kathy Miller understand the difficulty of change. In their book *When the Honeymoon's Over,* they wrote this about change: "Because each of us is affected by our own family of origin, it's hard for us to comprehend living any other way. When we begin dating that special person, our eyes begin to open somewhat to another way of living, but it's as if gauze covers our perception. We can't quite imagine that we'll have to change our lifestyle."[1]

The simple truth is that getting married means changing yourself — because no matter how hard you try, you can't really change another person.

FIRST STEPS

What would you change about your spouse if you could?

Brian: Hanna is an introspective and thoughtful person and spends a lot of time deep in thought. Sometimes she's thinking so hard that she unknowingly tramples over me and my feelings. It's not something she does on purpose, but she can be inconsiderate sometimes. I love her thoughtfulness and wouldn't change that, but I would like it if her thinking were a little more outward focused.

Hanna: Mine is similar to that in some ways. I have a stronger personality than Brian and I'm more visionary in my thinking. When I come up with an idea, he often goes into figuring out how to make it happen — even if the thing I've thought of is totally out of the question. He won't just say no to me. He'll give up things for me to make me happy and to fix things in me that only God can fix. He denies himself for me and that makes me sad sometimes.

IN SUMMARY

Understanding where we come from as individuals is vitally important in marriage. To build a shared future, we need more than love — we need to understand and be aware of our past. Jack and Carole Mayhall, who have written about marriage and conduct marriage seminars across the country, say, "Part of the process of falling in love — and staying in love — demands a knowledge and understanding of the background of our partner. This awareness comes through hard work, communication, compromise, adjusting. And a giant helping of God's grace."[2]

It's really as simple as this: You can pay now or pay later. You can do the long and rewarding work of talking about your history — where you come from and what you expect — or you can wait until those issues just show up. And they will show up.

A friend of mine who has been married about three months told me today at lunch that even though he and his wife spent a lot of time talking about expectations and histories, they still have issues that surface from time to time. But instead of manifesting as explosions, they are more like "aha" moments that remind them of some basic things they already know are true. He said those things are easy to handle because they already know so much about where they come from.

∞

VOICE OF WISDOM

For Brad and Kim Oaster, the differences in their family backgrounds are huge — especially when you consider their parents' marriages and their families. Brad and Kim married young — he was nineteen and she was seventeen — and they've been married for nineteen years.

"My family was totally dysfunctional," Brad says, looking back. "My parents divorced when I was three years old. My dad remarried once. And my mom remarried more than once — I've lost track of how many times! Even though they were divorced more than thirty years ago, they still fight. The last fight they had was just recently when our son was graduating from high school. Who was coming, who was not coming — it was a mess."

"Unlike Brad's parents, my parents are still married," says Kim. "They'll be married for forty years this month."

The family differences don't end there.

"I'm the middle child," Brad says. "From my parents, I have an older and a younger sister. I also have a much younger brother and sister from my dad and stepmother, and a younger brother from my mom and one of her husbands."

"I had just one brother who died when I was fifteen years old," says Kim. "He was seventeen. But my extended family was big and we did a lot of things together — aunts, uncles, cousins. There were so many of us that there was a freedom to be yourself. Brad's family was more concerned with fitting the pattern and not breaking the mold. I wasn't really what his family was looking for."

Early in their marriage, Brad and Kim discovered that family differences can cause problems if they're not understood and dealt with.

"My dad is a really arrogant person," says Brad. "What he says is fact, whether it's right or wrong. For example, when I was sixteen years old, his paycheck didn't show up one week. He told me that I took it from the mail, and I knew there was no point in denying it. With my father, I got to the point where I admitted to everything. I figured that I'd get blamed for it anyway, so I might as well be quiet and not confront him and just move out as soon as I could. His check came in the mail the next day, but he never apologized for accusing me of stealing it or admitted that he was wrong. He says he's a believer, but his actions are totally contradictory with that.

"In our marriage, I carried those same behaviors with me. I wouldn't talk about things that bothered me with Kim. Then, when the situation blew up, I'd dump on her for stuff that had gone on for a long time."

Kim agrees. "For us, the issue could have gone back for years and could take days to come out completely. I thought that everything I was doing was wrong. There was no way to please Brad — even though things weren't really about me or what I was doing.

"Unlike Brad's parents, my parents were really verbal. They talked things out. And even though my dad is loud and a little gruff, he's not hurtful. I'm more forceful like my dad, so I would confront Brad. Then things would really get ugly."

So what helped them overcome their family differences and learn to deal with conflict effectively?

"After we'd been married for five years or so, we went to marriage counseling," says Kim. "We took the Myers-Briggs personality test and our results were totally different. For so long, Brad had convinced me that I was the one with the problems — and I did have things I needed to deal with — but his results were so extreme. Brad really didn't know what normal was, and that gave me sympathy and understanding for him."

Brad agrees. "I lived with my mom, my dad, an aunt, my grandmother. I went to a military boarding school. Nothing was stable except for the boarding school, and even that had a system you could beat if you learned how, which I did.

"Our married life was stressful too. We were having babies and I had my own business."

Even though the counseling taught Brad and Kim to handle their family backgrounds, their families didn't change.

"Kim's family just approaches life differently," Brad says. "Her dad told me to learn a trade and get in a union and earn a pension. My response was 'Shoot me now!' That's not who I am — they didn't understand me at all. I don't think they understand me today, but we do get along."

Brad and Kim's oldest son, Jeremy, is thinking of getting married soon. So what advice would they offer him?

"Leave and cleave," says Kim. "You have to create your own life and your own family."

Brad agrees. "If we had just left the state and gone somewhere else, our parents would have viewed us differently when we came back."

"We lived close to my parents when we were first married," Kim says. "My parents were really careful to stay away even though we lived close by. That helped set some boundaries between us and them."

They'd also recommend counseling if necessary.

"Last fall, we had our first fight where we just talked it out," says Kim. "It took us nineteen years to get there, and counseling played a big part in that. I also had a mentor who told me that I didn't have to bring something up right away — especially if Brad had had a bad day. I could sit on it for a while.

"It's hard because I want to settle things right away. Brad wants to cool off first. I've learned to give him space — that really helps."

Brad laughs. "The most difficult thing we've dealt with is that I want to bury things like I did as a kid, and Kim follows me down the hallway wanting to resolve it right away.

"One of our worst fights centered around our son — it wasn't even between Kim and me. I was livid with him — a ten on a scale from one to ten — and didn't want him anywhere near me. I figured I could cool off and deal with it in the morning without hurting him."

"I didn't let it sit," says Kim. "I brought our son into the room so they could talk it out — just a minute or two after they'd argued. I saw Brad's face and realized that I just needed to back off and that was the start of learning that I need to give Brad some space."

"We really had to understand that our families affected how we try to resolve things," Brad says. "I want to resolve something in my head first — I'm very black and white. Kim wants to talk it out and deal with it out loud."

Things went from bad to worse for a while, but they didn't give up.

39

"I refused to give up," says Brad. "My mom and dad hated each other in front of us kids. Our family was broken, and there's no way I was going to let my kids grow up in a divorced family."

"It took me a while to understand that Brad was really committed to staying together," says Kim. "For a six-month period it was so miserable. We just went to bed without saying that we loved each other. All I heard from Brad was that things weren't working.

"My parents were so supportive during that time. There were nights where I'd be up all night crying while we argued. My mom would call in the morning and say, 'Your dad and I have been up praying all night for you. What's going on?' They helped with the children, but never interfered."

40

As they worked through their family differences and learned to handle conflict effectively, Brad and Kim saw God at work in their lives.

"People came to our wedding and gave us five years," says Brad.

"We renewed our vows when we'd been married for ten years," Kim says. "People stood up and talked about the grace they had seen in our marriage. We know that God has been the force that kept us together."

DISCUSSION QUESTIONS

- How has your family influenced your view of marriage?*

- What are some things you admire about your spouse's view of marriage, including some things you'd like to emulate from your spouse's parents?*

- How are your families similar? How are they different?

- How has divorce influenced your ideas about marriage? Did your parents get divorced? Your friends' parents?

- Describe your parents' marriage. What roles did they assume? How did they show each other they cared?*

- What are some boundaries that you need to set as a couple?*

- What was mealtime like in your family? What do you expect mealtimes to be like in your marriage?

- Read Genesis 2:24 again. Why do you think God commanded the man — and not the woman — to leave his father and mother? How do you think your relationships with your parents will change as you settle into marriage and begin to establish your own family?*

- Did you have pets as a child? Do you plan to have pets as a couple?

- What kinds of vacations did you take as a child? Do you want to take the same kinds of vacations with your spouse?

41

- Are you the firstborn in your family? A middle child? The baby? How do you think that has shaped who you are?

- Do you want to have children? How many? When?

- Did your family have a lot of company? How did that affect your family?

- How is your education similar to that of your spouse? How is it different? Do you think those differences will cause problems? Why, or why not?

- How do you plan to divide chores around the house?

42

---

* *Questions ideal for journaling*

CHAPTER TWO

How You Relate

COMMUNICATION

*T*OBEN:

Genesis 2 describes a time when everyone on earth spoke the same language. They got together and decided to build a great city with a tower that reached into the heavens. God took a look at what they were up to and was displeased.

He said, "If as one people speaking the same language they have begun to do this, then nothing they plan to do will be impossible for them. Come, let us go down and confuse their language so they will not understand each other.... That is why it was called Babel — because there the LORD confused the language of the whole world" (Genesis 2:6-7,9, NIV).

Our first apartment might have been called Babel as well.

"Je ne parle pas français." That means "I don't speak French." Joanne and I lived in Paris after we graduated from college. Joanne spoke French fluently, while I had barely squeaked through a couple of semesters of French in college. I would begin every interaction with every French person I talked to with the above sentence; then I would

plow ahead with a combination of bad French, English spoken with a French accent, and a couple of Spanish words that stuck with me from high school. Oh yeah, and I always spoke loudly.

I can't imagine what I must have inadvertently said to the lady at the grocery checkout or to the waiter at the restaurant around the corner from our apartment. "I would very much like to be eating one of your chicken house underwear tea kettle. Gracias." If I listened closely enough, spoke as carefully as I could, and asked for forgiveness, I could get by okay. When I didn't pay attention and spoke quickly, things were a mess.

I wonder now why, early in our marriage, I didn't think to start every conversation with "I don't know how to speak your language, but I will listen closely, speak as carefully as I can, and ask for forgiveness in advance." I think we would have avoided many misunderstandings, foibles, and hurt feelings if I had.

Joanne and I speak the same language today. It is a language that we have created together over the last ten years. We understand each other perfectly — most of the time. Occasionally, and with ever-decreasing frequency, we slip into our native tongues — and it's like Babel all over again.

WHAT IS COMMUNICATION?

In a nutshell, communication is the transfer of information from one person to another. Sounds simple enough, but most of the time it's not. Here's a basic model: In every act of communication there is a sender, a receiver, a message, and a context in which the message occurs.

The sender "encodes" a message. That means he thinks up what he wants to say. Then he sends it — speaks it out loud. The message is delivered in a context — time, place, atmosphere, and so on. The receiver then "decodes" the message. That means she interprets what was said, taking into account the context. Then it starts all over again.

There are a few places in this model where things can get significantly weird. Things like inflection, tone, and body language can cloud the meaning of the intended message. Context can certainly cause confusion too. It's a little like the game of telephone we all played when we were children. The sender is like the first person who whispers a phrase into someone's ear. The receiver is like the last person in the line who says what she heard. Context is like all the other little kids in the line who mess up the original phrase. No wonder what the receiver ends up hearing isn't always what the sender intended.

The Queen of Meta-Message

I don't think I would be out of line if I told you that early in our marriage Joanne had a tendency to meta-message. In fact, she was the meta-message queen. If you're not familiar with this term, let me break it down for you. When you meta-message, what you hear isn't quite what the other person said. It involves reading a different meaning into what you're hearing the other person say.

Picture this: It's Sunday morning, and it's about time to leave for church. Joanne has changed clothes a couple of times and is starting to get a little edgy. "I don't have anything to wear" is starting to sound like a Gregorian chant. She comes out of the bedroom for the fifth time, and here's how the conversation goes:

Joanne: What about this outfit?

Toben: I like it. Of course the one you had on before this one was great too.

Joanne: You don't like this one?

Toben: No, it's fine. I just think I like the other one better.

Joanne: So I should change?

Toben: No, you look fine.

Joanne: But you just said you don't like this dress.

Toben: No, I think it's fine. I just like the other one better.

Joanne: You do hate this dress. I knew it.

46   And on it goes. Joanne changes clothes a few more times and ends up heading out the door with the outfit she had on first. We're late for church, and the day is off to a gloomy start.

You get the picture. That's the dreaded meta-message. The person receiving the message interprets it and adds his or her own experience, understanding, insecurity, and even suspicion to its meaning until the original message is changed — sometimes to the point that what is heard is the polar opposite of what was intended.

To be fair, I've done my fair share of meta-messaging too. It's easy to do. At the very core of all this is a lack of trust that the person speaking really can be taken at his word. That's why meta-messaging is so dangerous in a new marriage.

Meta-messaging doesn't just affect things like what you're going to wear. Did you see the episode of *Friends* when Rachel and Ross decided to "take a break"? To Rachel, that meant some time to cool off and regroup. To Ross, it meant the relationship was over. Then Ross went out with the girl from the copy place and when Rachel found out, she was furious: "I said 'take a break,' not 'break up!'"

What means one thing to one person often means something totally different to someone else.

Joanne and I still meta-message from time to time, but over the years we've come to trust each other enough to take what we say at face value. If I tell Joanne she looks nice, that's really what I mean.

A Question of Style

Joanne and I dress differently. Just like Marie was a little bit country and Donny was a little bit rock-and-roll, Joanne is a little bit preppy/classic and I am a little bit trendy/nightmare. She is khaki skirts, sleeveless tops, and Kenneth Cole sandals to my baggy khaki shorts, ratty T-shirts, and chunky Adidas. When we walk down the mall together, people probably assume we're just two strangers walking near each other.

In the same way, our communication styles are different. I am verbose, to say the least. I love to talk. I'm loud and enthusiastic, with a good measure of cynicism and irony thrown in. I'm not a great listener, and I think on my feet very well. Joanne is more thoughtful and focused in the way she communicates. She's a fantastic listener and takes time to process things before she responds. So, figuratively speaking, how do we avoid looking like two strangers walking near each other?

Aretha Franklin sang it best: R-E-S-P-E-C-T. Sounds simple, right? I have to respect the fact that Joanne communicates in a very different way than I do. Not better, not worse, just different. And she has to do the same for me. Of course, as a result of the respect that we have for

47

each other's communication styles, our own styles have changed a little over the years.

Early on, I would give Joanne about two seconds to respond to something before I charged ahead. I ended up delivering a lot of monologues that were intended as dialogues. That's changed. I know Joanne sometimes needs a little more time to respond to something. But that amount of time is shorter than it used to be. Some of that quick processing has rubbed off on her; now she can speak her mind without weighing the consequences as much as she used to. In the same way, I'm learning to listen more carefully and to think a little longer before I speak.

Incidentally, there are some basic techniques both of you can use to help the communication process along. One: *Practice repeating each other,* especially in the midst of talking about a difficult or confusing issue. Telling your spouse, "This is what I hear you saying . . ." gives him or her a chance to clarify. Two: *Practice good listening skills.* Not interrupting shows the other person that you value them. Three: *Ask questions.* If you're not sure what your spouse really means, ask. Remember, there's no such thing as a dumb question (or so the saying goes). Four: *Put it in print.* If you're having a hard time communicating something to your partner, write it down. Sometimes it's easier to think on paper.

By the way, when it comes to communication, as well as a lot of other issues in marriage, taking a personality test together (if you haven't already) can be a real eye-opener. A number of online tests are available. Just type "personality test" in your search engine.

First Steps

How would you describe your communication style?

Hanna: Succinct. We had a fight the other day about a movie we were going to see. I said something quickly off the top of my head that was biting. And when I didn't want to see the movie Brian wanted to see I started acting angry. When I'm too succinct — especially in conflict — we go through a resolution where we have a period of letting the other person know how we're feeling. Then we try to determine why we said what we said that hurt the other person. Then we apologize and come to an understanding.

Brian: Listening-based. My communication style involves a lot of question asking. I feel very convinced that the best way to escalate any problem is to assume that I know what's going on. So I try to be conscious about gathering as much information as I can.

The Grid of Experience

Our friends Rick and Deb got in a fight shortly after they were married. Rick ended the argument quickly and brutally by suggesting that maybe they should just divorce and save themselves the trouble of future heated arguments. Deb was devastated. The only time she had heard those words was when her father said them to her mother. Her parents separated and divorced immediately thereafter. For her, divorce was not a joke, not something to be taken lightly. When Rick said those words, it brought back a flood of scary and painful emotions.

Philosopher Immanuel Kant would have had a field day with the above scenario. Kant proposed that we know things in two ways: We know something unto itself, and we know it through our experience of it. The word "divorce" can be viewed as a concept void of context, but in Deb's mind it couldn't be separated from her experience of it, which was when her dad left her mom.

This is a critical concept in marriage. For each of us, our experience of something (whatever it is at the moment) is guaranteed to be different, even if just slightly, from that of our spouse. Until you have a few years together in which you create shared experience, this can cause some strain. As time passes, you will come to a common understanding of what things mean. You will create your own definitions.

50 Here's another way to describe what I mean, as told by Larry and Kathy Miller: "We speak, and we hear our spouse's words through the filter of our own thinking, woven of the filaments of low self-esteem, insecurity, our temperament, and past traumatic experiences. As the comments of our mate pass through this filter, we interpret those comments based on our own viewpoint."[1]

Defining your terms as you go may seem like a forced exercise, but doing so — especially in the midst of conflict — can prevent unintentional misunderstandings and hurts. When Joanne and I were first married, her emotional vocabulary was a little stunted. My family talked about feelings and emotions all the time, whereas Joanne's family talked about those things less frequently.

I clearly remember a few times when Joanne would be visibly upset, with tears running down her face. I would ask her, "Are you sad?" and she would shake her head no. "But you're crying, so you must be sad," I'd insist.

Joanne's experience with emotions and how they had been defined in her family was very different from mine. To me, "sad" was tears rolling down your cheeks; to her, it meant something else. As we got to the heart of that matter, we worked to form some common meanings for our vocabulary so that "sad" meant the same thing to both of us.

*J*OANNE:

It wasn't necessarily that I wasn't sad — I was. But for me, learning how to express my feelings and learning that Toben really wanted to know them and to help was a long process. One of the biggest hurdles was realizing that I needed to answer with something other than "fine" when Toben asked me how I was doing. Usually, I was anything but fine when I insisted I was!

Do You Speak My Language?

Almost every weekend since we've been married, Toben takes my car to the gas station, fills it up with gas, and runs it through the car wash. So what does this have to do with communication?

Dr. Gary Chapman has identified five languages that express love: touching, talking, serving, giving gifts, and speaking encouraging words.[2] Each of us has a primary language that means love.

When Toben fills my car with gas, he's telling me loudly and clearly that he loves me. The primary way that he expresses his love for me is through service. Of course, I didn't understand this at first. *I wish he'd hold my hand more,* I'd think. *Then I'd really know that he loves me.* To me, touching meant love.

51

How does your partner communicate love? Does he do things for you, working hard to provide for your family? Or does he give you gifts to say he loves you? Does she enjoy long, intimate talks? Or does she give you a lot of hugs and back rubs?

What about you? How do you communicate love? I love to spend time talking with Toben. One of my favorite things to do on the weekend is to go for a long drive. I enjoy having the time to talk about all kinds of things, from what we did during the week to dreaming about our future. It's one of the ways that I communicate and receive love.

52 *T*OBEN:

After Audrey was born, I struggled as I tried to figure out my role as a husband and a father. Joanne's role was pretty evident. She breastfed Audrey and was able to comfort her in ways that I didn't seem capable of at the time. So in my confusion, I started to do a lot.

I thought the best way for me to show Joanne and Audrey that I loved them was to come home from work and take care of everything I could — take out the trash, unload the dishwasher, vacuum, cook, do laundry. You name it, I did it. I'd feel pretty good thinking I'd effectively shown them how much I loved them.

Turns out, Joanne's perception was quite different. She took all this activity as a lack of interest in Audrey and in her. What she wanted and needed was for me to spend time with them doing nothing. Just being there and available conveyed love to her.

It took us a few weeks, but we finally figured it out. Actually, Joanne figured it out and informed me what I was doing wrong! It took a little while for it to get through to me because I really felt like I was expressing my love in a good and valid way. But eventually I understood that what I thought was a good way to show love made Joanne feel just the opposite.

Joanne:

It wasn't that I didn't appreciate all that Toben was doing. I did. But somehow in all of his busyness I felt like Audrey and I were just in the way. We were obstacles to run the vacuum around! I was so amazed by this new little person in our lives that I could sit and stare at her for hours. And I wanted to see Toben express his love for her (and for me) by spending time with us.

53

First Steps

What says "I love you" to you?

Hanna: When Brian tries to change something because he knows it bugs me. Or when he learns something to please me. For example, we use several washcloths in the kitchen, and each one has a different purpose. He's gone out of his way to learn which is which and use them for their intended purpose. That means a lot to me.

Brian: When Hanna does something totally unexpected for me. Before we were married I came home at 3 A.M. from a horrible day and discovered that Hanna had come in and completely cleaned my room. It was wonderful!

ACTIONS SPEAK LOUDER THAN WORDS

In addition to the love languages that Dr. Chapman describes, it's important to look at body language. How we move and use our bodies speaks volumes.

I am a champion eye-roller. Growing up, I knew that rolling my eyes would get me in trouble — but I couldn't help it! It was almost second nature to me to roll my eyes when I heard something I thought was dumb or off base. Just the other day while we were taking a walk around the park, Toben caught me rolling my eyes at something he said. I hadn't said a word, but I had communicated all too clearly that I thought he was completely crazy.

Fortunately, Toben has a great sense of humor. Instead of getting upset or taking offense, he immediately exaggerated my action and asked me to give him lessons on how to roll his eyes as well as I do. (Of course, it takes years of practice, so it'll be a while before he's in my league!)

Our body language and facial gestures can communicate positive emotions as well. Have you ever looked at your partner across a room and known exactly what he was thinking? Jack and Carole Mayhall say that just looking at each other can develop intimacy in a couple:

Another way to develop the climate of intimacy in our relationships is by frequent glances at our spouses. This is one way to tell if an engaged couple is really in love with each other. Every joke, profound remark, or inane statement is a cause to glance at the other and share a look. Sadly, most couples begin to lose this eye contact after they have been married only a few months. If you have grown less frequent in the deep, long, intimate looks or the quick, let's-share-this look, talk about it and begin to glance at each other often when in group discussion (or even watching television). If the other doesn't glance back, give a nudge (if you're close enough) and soon you may again enjoy the warm feeling of sharing these intimate moments.[3]

I think it's fair to say that in addition to the primary love language we speak, most women need a lot of affection. I'm sure I'm not the only woman who has wished that we were as affectionate now as we were while we were dating. Kathy and Larry Miller wrote about this in their book *When the Honeymoon's Over:*

When Larry and I were dating, Larry frequently held my hand, put his arm around me, and made me feel loved and important. When he expressed his love in that way publicly, I felt secure. After we were married, my Prince Charming rarely held my hand or put his arm around me. I was shocked. I began keeping track of how often he failed to hold my hand. That only made me bitter.

Larry responded:

After the wedding, who in their right mind would prefer holding hands to making love? I believed affection before marriage was just the means to getting the "real stuff" later, and somehow sex would replace the inferior hand holding. However, over the years I've learned to enjoy giving Kathy the affection she needs and deserves.[4]

Of course, Toben's not the only one in our marriage who can give affection. I can too! As I crave affection, I've started to hold his hand more when we're driving in the car or taking a walk, and he's started doing the same in response!

*T*OBEN:

So many things changed from the time when we were dating to when we got married. While we were dating, Joanne didn't have a car at college for me to fill up on the weekends. We didn't have a house to fix up or a garage to keep clean. And we didn't have the time together that we now have as a married couple.

During our dating years, the time that we did have together was intensely focused on *being together*. We were so in love and wanted every moment together to count. I remember great conversations, walks around campus, time at the lake, late-night trips to Safeway for Ben & Jerry's, and the fact that most of the time we couldn't keep our hands off each other.

After we were married the distractions started to creep in. There were "things to do around the house." And I think we started to take for granted the time we had together. It started to get too easy to sit in front of the TV together or rent a movie.

The reality is that the more we took our time together for granted, the more we suffered relationally. Every once in a while, tension would build up until something (or someone) snapped. We would realize after talking it out that we needed to spend some "quality time" together. We would really focus on each other for a while. We would take walks, go to the lake, or sit on the couch and talk.

But before long we would fall back into those old, lazy patterns. That cycle continues to repeat for us today. For the most part we catch it before it gets critical and we adjust to focus more on each other, but it requires constant mindfulness. Filling up the car with gas just doesn't cut it.

Joanne knows that when I do that it's my way of saying "I love you." But I need to say "I love you" in ways that are more meaningful to her. And the only way I can be sure I am doing it right is to ask her. Even after being married for a few years, there's just no substitute for my asking, "What would make you feel loved?" Usually her answer is something incredibly simple like, "Come here and kiss me." So it works out well for both of us!

57

Talking to Others

*J*OANNE:

Let me brag about my husband for just a minute. Toben loves me. You know how I know? Not just because he tells me, but also because he tells everyone else that he loves me. Just yesterday, he came home from running errands with a friend. "I love you, Joanne," he said. "And I told Kevin all about how much I love you."

Occasionally I travel with Toben on business. When I meet people he has worked with, they always comment on how much Toben loves me and how wonderful he thinks I am.

In the New Testament, James has a lot to say about the power of words. This verse especially stands out to me: "Friends, don't complain about each other. A far greater complaint could be lodged against you, you know" (James 5:9).

His command is simple: Don't complain about each other. Toben never complains about me to other people. I wish I could say the same is true for me. But it's so easy to complain. I couch it in humor, laugh while I say it, but it's complaining nonetheless. "I just don't understand it," I say to another mother. "Toben hears Audrey wake up from her nap and just sits there. I'm determined not to get up — I've been with her all day. How can he not understand that it's his turn to take care of her? Is he deaf?"

Toben is a great father, and that's what I want to communicate to other people. How much better to keep my complaint — no matter how small — to myself and instead use my words to build up my husband in the eyes of others. How much better to use my words to show others what a loving and caring man he is.

I was visiting with some friends recently and one of them recounted a conversation she'd had with her husband. Filled with profanity, tinged with bitterness, and laced with sarcasm, it made me cringe. I've never met her husband and I'm sure he isn't the man she described him to be, but that's what comes to my mind whenever she mentions his name.

How often do I do the same? How often do I complain about something minor that colors someone's view of my spouse? How often have I spoken when I should have been silent? How would I feel to have those words come back to Toben?

Earlier in his letter, James described how words can come back to haunt us:

A bit in the mouth of a horse controls the whole horse. A small rudder on a huge ship in the hands of a skilled captain sets a course in the face of the strongest winds. A word out of your mouth may seem of no account, but it can accomplish nearly anything — or destroy it!

It only takes a spark, remember, to set off a forest fire. A careless or wrongly placed word out of your mouth can do that. By our speech we can ruin the world, turn harmony to chaos, throw mud on a reputation, send the whole world up in smoke and go up in smoke with it, smoke right from the pit of hell (James 3:3-6).

The smallest words can do huge damage. Words about our spouse can throw mud on their reputation that doesn't easily wash off.

FIRST STEPS

What is something you'd like to tell the world about your spouse?

Hanna: He's a great listener.

Brian: She's not as conservative as you might think. As the daughter of a contractor, she's heard it all and comes from a family who, more than any other family I've encountered, knows how to have a really fun time no matter where they are. She tends to present herself in a very put-together, somewhat conservative way, when really she is able to cut loose at a moment's notice, have a ton of fun, and just be nuts.

WHATEVER IS TRUE

*T*OBEN:

When Joanne and I were engaged, we were both working on our "stuff." Joanne was in counseling, and I was not always as supportive as

I should have been. I remember one occasion in particular when we were walking across campus to the dining hall for lunch. It was a beautiful fall day, the leaves were changing on the trees, and the air was cool.

Between Joanne's dorm and the doors of the cafeteria I took the opportunity to tell her a few more things I thought she should work on in her upcoming appointment with her counselor. I got right to the point, outlining the obvious problems she needed to address and how important it was that she take seriously the baggage she was carrying, because she was about to carry it into *our* marriage.

Fortunately, she was not armed or I would have been a dead man. She had been working hard for months on some difficult and painful issues. Instead of telling her how proud I was of the work she had done and how excited I was for the both of us that she was committed to seeing it through, I plowed ahead with my laundry list.

Though she wasn't packing a pistol, she did the one thing that she knew would level me. She took off her engagement ring and flung it at my head. Then she turned around and ran back to her dorm room. I stood there holding the ring thinking to myself, "I blew it!" The point wasn't whether what I had said was true — Joanne would tell you that she still had some work to do — but how and when I said it was completely *wrong*.

*J*OANNE:

The truth can hurt. That's why we're commanded to speak the truth in love (see Ephesians 4:15). So what does that look like?

I recently heard a woman on television giving advice to a mother who constantly nagged her children. "Every time you say something negative," she said, "I want you to say five positive things to go along with it." It might not be hard to say five nice things. Unfortunately the word "but" can erase them all. A friend of mine told me that her child's karate instructor took a different approach by saying, "Good . . . now. . . ." That makes you say the positive thing and then build on it. Pretty good advice that works in marriage too. For example, saying, "It's great that you wash the dishes, but why don't you ever dry them?" wipes out the compliment. But saying, "It's great that you wash the dishes, now if you would dry them too it would really help me out," leaves you both feeling great.

Now, I don't know about you, but when I'm good and mad, I have a hard time thinking anything nice about the person I'm mad at. Never mind that Toben is the love of my life; when I'm upset, I'm ashamed to say that I have a hard time thinking of even one nice thing about him. So how can I learn to speak the truth in love?

I think Paul has the answer. In Philippians he writes this: "Summing it all up, friends, I'd say you'll do best by filling your minds and meditating on things true, noble, reputable, authentic, compelling, gracious — the best, not the worst; the beautiful, not the ugly; things to praise, not things to curse" (4:8).

What's true about your spouse? In what ways is she authentic? How is he gracious? What do you love best about her? What beauty attracted you to him in the first place?

If we fill our minds with the best, most beautiful, and most praise-worthy things about our spouses, that's what will come out of our mouths. Jesus said as much to His disciples in Matthew 15:18-19: "But what comes out of the mouth gets its start in the heart. It's from the

61

heart that we vomit up evil arguments, murders, adulteries, fornications, thefts, lies, and cussing." By the same token, if we fill our hearts with positive things, that's what will come out — even when we're good and mad.

IN SUMMARY

When it comes right down to it, good communication is all about choice. I can choose to keep silent, choose to say something positive, or choose to say something hurtful. Making good communication choices isn't easy and doesn't come naturally, but it is possible.

Remember that communication is affected by a huge variety of things — from your surroundings or the time of day (Toben and I have had any number of conversations late at night that I don't remember at all in the morning!) to past experiences and body language.

Spend some time talking together about how you communicate, and pray that God would use your words to build up one another and to express how much you love and care for each other.

∽

VOICE OF WISDOM

Steve and Darlene Hixon have been married for twenty-one years. These two obviously love each other a lot. The first time I (Joanne) met them was at a potluck for a Bible study that Toben attends with Steve. Part of the evening's "entertainment" was a poetry reading — each husband wrote a poem about his wife to introduce her to the group.

Steve's poem was filled with inside references that demonstrated their history together and the importance communication has played in their relationship. We had breakfast with them recently and talked with them about communication in their marriage.

Toben: What comes to your mind when you think about communication in your marriage?

Steve: When we were first married, I remember that we would have breakfast together every Saturday. I was going to seminary and Darlene was working for American Express. We were busy, leaving early in the morning and filling our evenings with a lot of activity. We were involved in a fellowship group of single people before we were married, and it was important to us that we didn't stop doing that after we came back from our honeymoon. So Saturday mornings were a time for us to connect.

Darlene: We were very involved with other people, and it was a good thing. Our relationships remained the same and our pace remained the same after we were married.

Steve: We both wanted that.

63

Darlene: We didn't want to lose our friends or cocoon. And we didn't want to lose relational accountability. In some ways, marriage was not so different for us than being single.

Joanne: I think some people expect they'll be completely different people after they get married. I know I did.

Darlene: Having kids is more different than getting married. You can almost keep your same lifestyle after you get married that you had before. Not so with kids.

Toben: Were your family communication styles very different?

Darlene: They were totally opposite! My family was like an Italian Mafia scene at every meal — breakfast, lunch, and dinner. My parents used the dinner table as a battleground. The great thing was that no one was mad after those meals. That's just what a discussion looked like in my family. When Steve joined the family it was like Cher and Nicolas Cage in *Moonstruck*.

So when we got married, I'd come in and scream and yell, and Steve just didn't say anything.

Steve: My family was more like the Cleavers. It wasn't totally closed down and uptight, but it seemed that way compared to Darlene's family. The thing that was really different was our fighting styles. Hers was explosion; mine was sweep it under the rug.

Joanne: So were you intentional about coming up with a communication style that was uniquely yours?

Darlene: No, not really.

Steve: It was mostly a problem with conflict. That's where we would see our communication suffer. I would stuff things and hang on to them for days and days. Darlene would explode and then it was over. Over the years I've learned to explode and she kept exploding.

Darlene: I remember a friend of ours telling us that they learned how to have a healthy fight. But it was a process. For me, learning healthy communication in conflict was realizing that I could be abusive, and for Steve, it was learning that he just shut down.

Toben: How long did it take for you to feel like you hit your stride in your communication? When did it start to smooth out?

Steve: We were living in an apartment at the time . . .

Darlene: . . . and I can still see my heel marks in the door!

Steve: That was from the new rule that you couldn't leave the room angry.

Darlene: You couldn't exit the geographic area. That wasn't okay with me. I got so mad at being stuck with him in that room that I kicked the door. It took a while, but it got smoother. I think that, for us, communication was fine until we hit a conflict. That's where things could get ugly.

Steve: At the time, I think we thought my family was the healthy one and hers was the unhealthy one. She was really trying to get away from her family.

Joanne: Do you still feel like that's the case?

Darlene: Now I don't think we'd want to be like my family or his family. As you get older, you realize what mistakes you made and gain perspective on your families.

Steve: For example, my dad decided to move to Arizona after living thirty years where they were. He bought a house there and didn't even ask my mom whether she wanted to move.

Toben: Were there other couples you emulated?

65

Steve: Yes. After I became a Christian I was really impressionable. Steve and Sally in particular gave me hope for communication in marriage. I saw them being open about absolutely everything and fighting fairly.

Joanne: What topics are difficult for you to communicate about?

Darlene: Finances are number one. In fact, it may be the only one.

Steve: I agree. It's a pretty short list.

Darlene: Back in the beginning of our relationship our styles of communication were a process to get used to. I was used to nonverbal cues, but I didn't get any from Steve. He was very reserved. In the first year of our marriage I was really looking for those nonverbals — and they just weren't there.

Steve: We had style issues. I liked Darlene's style but it was a different style than I had or had seen in my family. And after a while it started to bug me.

Joanne: It's interesting that often the things that attract us to our spouse turn out to be the things that bug us in the end.

Steve: Another thing we dealt with in communication was that we expected the worst of each other when it came to making decisions. For example, when we went to look for apartments I took us to one worse than I wanted to live in because I knew that she would want to go up a couple of levels from wherever we were. And Darlene looked at apartments significantly nicer than what she expected to live in because she knew I would bring it down a few notches.

Darlene: We've learned to start in the middle more often and to expect the best of the other person — to say what we mean and to believe the other person means what he or she says too.

Discussion Questions

- Have you taken a personality test in the past? What did you learn from it?

- Do you usually get right to the point in a conversation, or do you prefer to get to it eventually?

- Are you an introvert or an extrovert? Are you energized by being alone or with people?

- Do you tend to meta-message? What are some ways you could stop?

- What are some of the things you love most about your partner? How can you fill your mind with those things?*

- What messages does your body language send to your spouse? Answer for yourself and for your spouse, and then compare answers.

- Are there certain words or phrases that have totally different meanings to you and your partner? What are they? What experiences shaped those meanings?

- How would you describe your communication style?

- How do your communication styles differ? How are they similar?*

- What's one thing about the way your parents communicate that you'd like to emulate? One thing you would do differently?*

- Are you more likely to point out a strength or a weakness in your partner?

- If you have something important to tell your spouse, would you rather tell him or her face-to-face or write a letter?

- What's something you have a hard time communicating to your spouse? Why is it so difficult?*

- What language do you use to communicate love? What language communicates love to your spouse? How can you learn to speak his or her love language?*

- Do you think gender affects communication style? If so, how?

- What was the best conversation you've ever had with your spouse? What made it so good?

---

* *Questions ideal for journaling*

CHAPTER THREE

How You Resolve Conflict

FIGHTING FAIRLY

JOANNE:

We'd just returned from our honeymoon in Carmel, California. It was January and we were moving into our tiny student apartment on campus. Neither of us was taking a class for the month-long term, and we were unpacking boxes, listening to music, and enjoying the process of setting up our little home.

Enjoying it, that is, until I walked into the bathroom.

There on the floor and the counter were all the towels and linens I had just folded and put away in the linen closet. I took a deep breath and let it out. "What are you doing?" I asked — calmly, I thought.

"I'm folding all the towels the right way," Toben said.

That did it. "What do you mean the *right* way?" I asked through clenched teeth. "They *were* folded the *right* way. I spent an hour this morning putting everything away in there and you've just undone it all. How could you?"

There you have it. Our first married fight. Pretty dumb, but I thought it was the end of the world. We'd only been married a couple of weeks and we couldn't even agree about folding towels. What would happen when we started to share a tube of toothpaste? I was sure we'd never make it.

DAIRY QUEEN AND GOING AROUND CORNERS

Most of the fights we've had as a couple have been over stupid things. And we're not alone. I was talking with one friend recently who told me that one of the first fights she and her husband had was about Dairy Queen. They'd been driving through Texas on their way to visit family and she'd mentioned she wanted to stop at the next DQ they passed. He kept driving. *He doesn't love me anymore,* she thought.

These kinds of fights sound silly, but — for us anyway — it seems like the fights about little things are always the worst. Yesterday at dinner we were talking with my parents about this. They agreed that the majority of disagreements they've had have been over stupid things too — things like how you spread dirt in the garden or hang wallpaper. Often we don't take these conflicts seriously because they're not really important. But the habits we use in these little disagreements set a pattern for how we react when big issues arise. That's why little arguments are a great place to start when it comes to building conflict resolution skills.

Before Toben and I were engaged, his parents bought him a car. For the longest time, he wouldn't let me drive it. And when he did — on the way to visit some friends of his parents for dinner — we got into the biggest fight we'd had so far.

I made a right turn on the way to the gas station. From my perspective, there was plenty of room between the car and the curb. But from Toben's vantage point, it was entirely too close. He yelled, we pulled into the gas station, and I was removed from the driver's seat.

By the time the gas was pumped and we were on our way, I was mad. My feelings were hurt, but I couldn't get the words out to describe why. Toben pushed for an explanation for my stony silence, but I refused to answer. (Unfortunately, I was — and sometimes still am — great at silence that speaks volumes.) Halfway there, I finally managed to blurt out that my feelings were hurt, but that I needed a few minutes to understand why and that I couldn't talk about it yet.

We pulled over at a park, got on the swings, and the "Fifteen-Minute Time-Out Rule" was born. Toben promised that he wouldn't say a word for fifteen whole minutes. (And at that point, this was unheard of for him!) We swung in silence, and when we got back into the car I was able to calmly explain why my feelings were hurt as well as able to listen and understand as Toben explained his side of the story.

We don't use the "Fifteen-Minute Time-Out Rule" very much anymore, but it helps me immensely to know it's there if I need it. And it saved a lot of hurt feelings and words that couldn't be taken back during our early years of marriage.

I hate to admit it, but when I start feeling backed into a corner, I lash out. I say mean, hurtful, and ugly things that I end up regretting. And as Meg Ryan's character said in *You've Got Mail,* there's no reason to say those kinds of things to someone — no matter what he's done (or what you think he's done) to deserve it. Paul said much the same thing in 1 Thessalonians: "And be careful that when you get on each other's nerves you don't snap at each other. Look for the best in each other, and always do your best to bring it out" (5:15).

Instead of snapping at Toben and lashing out to hurt him, I could call for time out and walk away — knowing that there was a set time for resolution.

LAUNDRY LISTS AND OTHER BAD THINGS

The reason the time-out rule works so well is that we're not really walking away from our disagreement — we're just postponing it for a while. Completely walking away from a fight never to return is not a good approach.

We've found that a few other things never work well when resolving conflict:

Bringing up the past. Have you heard this one? One man said, "When we quarrel, my wife becomes historical."

"Don't you mean hysterical?" his friend asked.

"Nope," the man replied. "When we fight, she reminds me of everything I ever did to her."

Bringing up things that are in the past is never a fair way to approach conflict resolution. In fact, instead of resolving conflict, you only add a bunch of other issues to be resolved, and you never get anywhere!

Exaggerating. I happen to be really good at this one — something I'm not very proud of. Especially when I know I'm in the wrong, I will blow whatever the issue is way out of proportion. Until I get the issue into a right perspective, it's not going to get resolved.

This even affects little things. One morning, I called downstairs for Toben and asked him to call the weather line so I could decide what to wear. He couldn't remember the number. "Two-three-oh or six-three-oh?" he asked. I answered, and he still dialed the number wrong. Frustrated, he told me never to yell down the stairs at him.

"Why?" I yelled. "You always do!" We'd moved into the house less than a week before. Some *always*.

Intimidating. Because of the way we approach conflict differently, Toben intimidated the heck out of me when we were first married. He came to discussions and conflicts armed with data, ready to defend his position. I've said before that that made me feel completely overwhelmed. I don't think I'd be out of line to say he was tempted to use that in his favor a time or two when we were first married. Tell your spouse (when you're not in a conflict) what he or she does that intimidates you. If your spouse tells you that you can be intimidating, be understanding of those things and don't use them to win a fight. Toben still can defend his position in an argument, but he doesn't hit me with all the research up front.

Giving up. It's never a good idea to give up on a disagreement. By giving up, you're telling your spouse the relationship isn't worth it. And that can't lead anywhere that's good. I'm ashamed to say this is something I fall back on all too easily when the discussion isn't going my way.

When we were first married, this usually involved me throwing up my hands and heading for the bathroom where I'd lock the door and ignore Toben's knocking. I know that sometimes it feels like there's something standing between you and your spouse in conflict, but adding a heavy door doesn't help.

Refusing to talk. This was my very favorite way to handle conflict. *If you don't agree with me or won't see things my way, I just won't talk to you,* I'd think.

73

But this just communicates the same thing as giving up: You're not worth my time and effort. Needless to say, it's hard to resolve conflict when only one person is talking.

Humiliating. I'm glad to say that Toben has never tried to humiliate me in the middle of a disagreement. I can't imagine what it would be like to be humiliated or put down while trying to resolve conflict.

Have you ever been in the awkward position of being around a couple who's fighting? It seems like humiliation is often a way to win a fight in front of others. One put-down in front of friends, and the person who has been humiliated folds.

74   *Changing the subject.* Have you ever tried to bring something up that needs to be discussed, only to have someone change the subject on you? How frustrating! If something needs to be resolved, there's no time like the present. It only gets harder the longer you wait to talk about it.

Often when Toben points out something in me that needs to change, I feel embarrassed and uncomfortable. One method I use to get out of the discussion is the "yeah, well, you do this or that that bugs me too" approach. Resolution can't happen until you're both talking about the same thing.

Interrupting. James writes, "Lead with your ears, follow up with your tongue, and let anger straggle along in the rear" (1:19). You can't listen to your partner's feelings and viewpoint if you're busy talking. Interrupting the other person to get your point across tells your partner that what he or she has to say isn't as important as what you want to say.

First Steps

What's your favorite way to turn the tables on your spouse in a disagreement?

Hanna: I tell him he's hurt my feelings. He's so concerned about them that he backs off.

Brian: I get passive-aggressive. I keep quiet or just walk away.

Win/Win Versus the Zero-Sum Game

*T*OBEN:

Let's define some terms. Win/win means we both win. In the zero-sum game, I don't care if I lose as long as you lose too. Of course win/win sounds like a good way to go, but in the heat of the moment, the zero-sum game has a way of creeping up on you.

I hate to use a boxing analogy in a marriage book, but I'll do it anyway. When a fighter is against the ropes getting the daylights pounded out of him, he knows he's going down. What would it matter if he were to throw a punch below the belt or bite someone's ear off? He's going to lose the fight anyhow; he might as well make his opponent pay.

The same thing has happened in our marriage from time to time. I tend to overwhelm Joanne when we get into disagreements, sometimes to the point that she feels suffocated. In order to save herself, she may go for the knockout punch.

There are definitely things that I have done in our married life that I am ashamed of. Some of them are so grievous to me that just the mention of them takes the air out of me. When Joanne is on the ropes, all she has to do is bring up one of these past mistakes and it's all over for me. Joanne wins by TKO (technical knockout). But the truth is that she doesn't really win because she feels terrible when she does it.

Believe it or not, the zero-sum game is a two-way street. There really isn't much excuse to go there, but if I'm relentless when Joanne and I disagree — if she feels like she has to pull out all the stops in order to survive — then I have it coming. So the key is for me to make sure I never, ever get her on the ropes. Even in our most vehement disagreements I need to give her room to breathe, room to escape so she doesn't have to go for the kill.

The win/win is just as wonderful as it sounds, but it takes a very focused and intentional effort to get there. One of the best examples of win/win occurs in Scripture when Jesus submitted to death on the cross. To many, Jesus' death looked like a win/lose. Many of His followers had expected Him to destroy their enemies and to reign here on earth. But that's not what happened.

Jesus honored His Father by dying, rising from the dead, and finally ascending into heaven to sit at His Father's right hand. He won. But so did everyone else. Because of His atoning work on the cross, we have the opportunity to spend eternity with Christ in heaven. Jesus' self-sacrifice turned what was intended for evil into the best thing that has happened in the course of human history.

Romans 6:6-10 says this:

Could it be any clearer? Our old way of life was nailed to the Cross with Christ, a decisive end to that sin-miserable life — no longer at sin's every beck and call! What we believe is this: If we get included in Christ's sin-conquering death, we also get included in his life-saving resurrection. We know that when Jesus was raised from the dead it was a signal of the end of death-as-the-end. Never again will death have the last word. When Jesus died, he took sin down with him, but alive he brings God down to us.

On a much smaller scale we can do the same thing in our marriage. Dying to self is a biblical concept and a very helpful way to get to win/win. When I lay down my life for Joanne, I show her that she is more valuable to me than I am to myself. That gives her a deep sense of security that makes it easier for us to work through an issue without damaging each other. When Joanne dies to herself, the same thing happens to me. She demonstrates how much she loves me and then I am willing to go to any length to work things out with her.

As easy as it is to go for the zero-sum game, it doesn't benefit anyone. But to have a win/win situation, you have to lay down some ground rules for conflict.

Fighting by the Rules

There are rules in every relationship, but most of them are unspoken. Having some "spoken rules" in place will aid you in your communication — especially in the midst of conflict.

Don't make "you" statements. Nothing puts me on the defensive the way the word "you" does. I like "I" statements much better. With practice you can get exactly the same idea across by saying "I" instead of "you."

For example, the other night I had to go to church to participate in a ministry I helped start a couple of months back. Joanne and I hadn't seen each other all day. She could have said, "You have too much going on to spend enough time with me." Had she said that, I would have chronicled all the reasons why I was doing what I was doing, and Joanne wouldn't have felt any better. Instead she said, "I miss you when you are gone all day and then have to go out in the evening too." I got the picture right away, and instead of feeling defensive, I felt valued.

Repeat what your partner just said. We mentioned this in the communication chapter, but it bears saying again. Often conflict is caused by misunderstanding. Try responding to everything your spouse says with "What I hear you saying is. . . ." Put what you heard into your own words and make sure you understood correctly what was said.

Last night Joanne made a chocolate cake — a flourless, gooey, amazing chocolate cake. I didn't have any. Today as she was getting a piece out for dessert after lunch, she asked me if I'd had any last night. "Oh no," I said. "I've had it before."

She immediately said, "It sounds like you're saying that you've had it before and therefore are sure not to have it again. Are you saying you don't like this cake?"

That's not what I meant at all. By taking the time to ask me what I meant, she avoided hurt feelings and I was able to restate what I meant, which was something like this: "No, I didn't have any last night. I've had it before and I know how good it is."

Use the "Time-Out Rule." Joanne talked about this rule earlier in the chapter, but it has been so valuable to us I thought I'd mention it in this list as well. Make sure you talk about how you're going to use your time-outs before you get into a sticky situation. When trouble is brewing you want to know that this rule is well defined so that both of you know what time-out means. Specifics might include how long the time-outs will last or if they are to be spent alone or together.

Once the rule is set, stick with it. When Joanne would call a time-out, I was obligated to shut up for at least fifteen minutes, during which I would get away from her so she had time to think. If, at the end of that time, she still needed some time to think, we would postpone the discussion, no matter how badly I wanted to talk about it, until a mutually agreed upon time later in the day or even later in the week. Which leads us to the next rule.

Set aside time to work through the tougher issues. Some issues are too emotionally charged for a time-out to help. It's okay to postpone those tough discussions long enough for everyone to cool off and think clearly about the issue at hand. Sometimes, when things were especially tense and we were busier than usual, Joanne and I would schedule a time (we would actually write it in our calendars) to discuss the issue later in the week. Don't put it off any longer than you have to, but make sure you give yourselves the time you need to come back to the issue with a fresh perspective and a resolve to work through it to a win/win solution.

A word of caution here: The Bible is clear that we're not to let the sun go down on our anger. Setting a tough issue aside is okay as long as both partners agree to do so and as long as you get back to it as soon as possible. However, this isn't an "out" if you're just not in the mood to work on your relationship.

Don't forget to have fun. Early in our marriage, Joanne and I had some tough stuff to deal with. It seemed like some weeks were just a series of time-outs and scheduled rematches. During those weeks, we were relationally ineffective because we were so emotionally exhausted that we couldn't make anything work. So there were times that we decided to put all the looming issues on the back burner and just have some fun. It can be tough to move aside the pressing issues in order to have fun. But every time we did it, we came back with a renewed enthusiasm to work things out.

I can remember a specific time when everything seemed to be falling apart. School was out of control. We were finishing our last semester of college and both taking a full course load. Joanne was working two jobs, and I was heavily involved in student government. Even though we ended up at the same place each night, we felt like our lives were completely separate. Dinner together had disappeared, and if we both happened to be home, one of us was working on a paper. We were starting to feel a little panicked about life after college and scared of not finding good jobs, and we had precious little time to talk about what we were feeling.

Joanne and I decided to forget about it all and go to Seattle for the weekend. We promised each other we wouldn't bring up any of the issues we'd been wrestling with. We had a great weekend, returned refreshed to our little apartment, and were able to work through our schedules, our fears, and our course load more effectively because of it.

Come up with your own rules and commit them to paper. Because every relationship is different, the rules that work best for you will probably be different from ours. As situations arise, make sure you think about what would make those circumstances better, and make a rule out of it. If you want to, put those rules on paper and put them on the fridge. That way you'll both be mindful of your rules and you'll feel the freedom to use them whenever they are needed.

At first, using your rules may seem awkward and forced, but it will get easier and easier. In time, you won't need them very often because they'll become an integrated part of how you communicate and resolve conflict.

FIRST STEPS

What's one of the rules you use in conflict with your spouse?
Brian and Hanna: We always finish what we start. We constantly ask, "Are you okay?"

NAME IT AND CLAIM IT

*J*OANNE:

Have you ever thought you were having an argument about where to have dinner when in reality you were arguing about something else? We have. So have Percy and Velma, characters in some of my favorite books, The Mitford Series, by Jan Karon:

> *Percy scribbled on the back of an order pad. "That's a hundred and fifty beef dogs, max, plus all the trimmin's, includin' Velma's chili —"*
>
> *"Wrong!" said Velma. "I'm not standin' over a hot stove stirrin' chili another day of my life! I've decided to go with canned from here out."*
>
> *"Canned chili?" Percy was unbelieving.*
>
> *"And how long has it been since you peeled spuds for french fries? Years, that's how long. They come in here frozen as a rock, like they do everywhere else that people don't want to kill theirselves workin'."*

"Yeah, but frozen fries is one thing, canned chili is another."

"To you, maybe. But not to me."

Velma stalked away. Percy sighed deeply.

The rector didn't say anything, but he knew darn well their conversation wasn't about chili.

It was about a cruise.[1]

Call us Percy and Velma. We've had a ton of fights about something minor when what was really bothering us was something bigger. For example, about a month ago I got on Toben's case for not fixing a baseboard that came loose. In fact, I really blew up at him over it. But what was bothering me was not so much that the baseboard was loose, but that he'd said he would fix it and hadn't. It had been a busy few weeks and there were several things he'd said he would do, but he hadn't done any of them. I was beginning to feel like I couldn't trust him or believe him when he promised me things because he didn't do what he said.

To benefit from conflict, you have to understand just what you're arguing about in the first place. Jack and Carole Mayhall have identified the following steps toward determining problems and making conflict constructive.[2]

Define the problem or area of disagreement. It sounds pretty simple, but sometimes defining the disagreement is a lot easier said than done. Take your time and discover if there's an issue behind your disagreement that needs to surface. Is it about canned chili or something else?

Instead of blowing up about the baseboard, I could have told Toben that when he doesn't do what he says he will do, I feel like I can't trust him and that he doesn't love me.

Recognize the ways you both contribute to the problem. Just as it takes two to tango, it takes two to disagree. Chances are, no matter how sure I am that something is all Toben's fault, I've played more than a supporting role in the conflict.

In the baseboard incident, I'd only asked Toben once to fix it. Even though I knew he was busy, I neglected to remind him, and he just plain forgot.

Brainstorm all possible solutions. This is something that Toben is really good at. From the completely wild to the very practical, he's great at ideas. Remember that in a brainstorm, every idea is as valid as the next. Determining which idea is the best comes later.

For us, the brainstorm on how to fix the baseboard problem   83
included things like me reminding Toben of things he said he'd do or making a "honey-do" list, and Toben writing things to be done on his calendar — on a specific day rather than just a general to-do list.

Discuss each solution and agree on one to try. Maybe it's not financially possible to fly off for a weekend in Paris to add more romance to your marriage. But what about filling your home with candlelight or taking time each week to go on a date? This is when you evaluate the ideas from your brainstorm and pick one that will work for both of you.

We chose to implement a combination of all three solutions. I remind Toben when something's really important to me and he writes things down.

Set a time to review your progress. It could be a day, a week, or a month later, but it's important to return to the issue and evaluate your solution. If it's working — great! If not, that's the time to go back to your brainstorm and pick a new idea to try.

One of the ways we've stayed on top of the things Toben has said he'll do is by talking over breakfast on Saturday mornings. As part of making our plans for the weekend, I remind Toben of the household things I'd like him to do. Then we talk about when they'll get done and how I can help.

The Mayhalls go on to give their own list of ground rules for fighting fairly.

Focus on the beautiful. Remember that this person is your "Mr. (or Mrs.) Right." You love this person and chose to spend the rest of your life together. This is one that I especially have to work on when Toben and I aren't getting along. It's so easy to get caught up in the disagreement that I forget just how much I love him. A quick glance at my wedding ring reminds me how excited I was when Toben proposed and how happy I was to marry him. Remembering helps me to focus on those things in him that made me fall in love in the first place.

Learn to communicate ideas and feelings more clearly. This was one that was hard for me to learn. I didn't think Toben would care about my feelings — especially if I was in the wrong. But he does care. And he's helped me learn how to describe to him what I'm feeling in a clear manner.

When we first started dating, I was amazed at all the ways Toben could describe his feelings. Colors, animals, weather, days of the week — you name it, he could apply them to feelings. It became a challenge for me to do the same. So now when I tell Toben that I feel like a rainy day, he knows I'm feeling pretty content, a little melancholy, and ready for some time alone.

Be very careful about venting hostile feelings. Words often seem to fly out of our mouths when we're unaware of them. Mom was right: Think before you speak — or act.

One of the most public fights Toben and I had was walking across campus to the dining hall. I don't even remember what started it. (Toben does. Remember his version of the story?) But I was feeling pressure to become an instantly perfect person. Without thinking, I blew up and threw my engagement ring at Toben's head before running back to my dorm room to cry. Poor Toben. I can't imagine how awful it must have felt to search for my ring among all the pine needles with so many people looking on.

Study your partner's differences. As you work through disagreements together, notice what makes your partner tick. I usually need some time to think about what I want to say. Toben has studied that and will usually suggest some quiet time before we discuss the problem. That has helped me approach our arguments without feeling defensive and scared.

Don't just limit your study of your partner to disagreements. Knowing your differences ahead of time can help you avoid conflict. Toben has learned that while I love to entertain, I don't like to do it unless the house is clean and I feel prepared. When we were first married, he once invited fifteen people for dinner and gave me a half-hour notice. A big conflict arose (although dinner came off smoothly at the last minute!). Now I'm more prepared for last-minute guests and Toben is more careful about giving me advance warning.

Never underestimate the power of praying together. God wants us to get along with each other. In Romans 12:16, Paul wrote, "Get along with each other; don't be stuck-up." There's nothing that helps me get over being stuck-up with Toben more than praying with him. As you disagree, ask God to help you come to an agreement.

As I try to think of an example from our marriage for this, I'm stuck. This is definitely easier said than done for us. Praying together means giving up the option to win. Instead, we're forced (in an ultimately good way) to look for a solution that satisfies both people.

Make physical contact. It's hard to argue when you're holding hands. I once read something that suggested taking off all your clothes and getting into the bathtub together when it's time to discuss a problem. Talk about making yourself vulnerable!

I don't know that we've ever gone that far, but Toben is good about sitting down and holding my hands. He's also great at looking me directly in the eye when we're talking about something difficult. It lets me know that he's concerned about me, and it makes me feel safe and loved.

Forgive — quickly. One wife described her unwillingness to forgive when she was first married and not getting along well with her husband: "I closed an inner door. Stubborn, stiff-necked, unwilling to let go. Unwilling to forgive. I wanted to hold on, to remember, to go over and over my hurt in my mind. I wanted to make him pay until I felt it was time, until I was ready. A pattern emerged."[3]

That's the scary part of not forgiving and forgetting — a pattern emerges that's difficult to break. We hang on to our hurts and bring the past with us into the future. Leave the past in the past. Once an issue is resolved, commit to leaving it in the past. Nothing is as hurtful as bringing up an issue your spouse thought was resolved.

Go beyond forgiveness to understanding. Take some time to understand what you were fighting about and how you resolved it. What worked? What didn't work? Remember those things the next time you find yourselves in a similar situation.

Remember You Love Each Other

Paul wrote that we're "chosen by God for this new life of love" — something that sounds a lot like marriage. But in the midst of conflict, it's easy to forget how much you love each other. To help you remember, focus on these wise words from Colossians 3:12-14:

> *So, chosen by God for this new life of love, dress in the wardrobe God picked out for you: compassion, kindness, humility, quiet strength, discipline. Be even-tempered, content with second place, quick to forgive an offense. Forgive as quickly and completely as the Master forgave you. And regardless of what else you put on, wear love. It's your basic, all-purpose garment. Never be without it.*

In Summary

*T*OBEN:

Conflict in marriage is inevitable. But conflict in marriage isn't necessarily bad. Don't get me wrong; I don't think it's a wonderful thing you should practice often. But I do think it has a good side.

Conflict can be viewed as an isolated event or as a process. It's the process part of conflict that's worth valuing. In any disagreement there are two key elements: the issue at hand and the way it's addressed. No matter what the issue is — whether it's how to fold towels or whether to stop at Dairy Queen — the way it's addressed can be the same.

The next time you're in a disagreement, take some time to think about how you address challenging issues. Do you listen to your partner's point of view? Do you remember to treat your spouse lovingly — no matter how strongly you disagree? Conflict provides an opportunity to love your mate in the midst of difficult circumstances.

∞

VOICE OF WISDOM

Psychologist Tom Whiteman is a director for Fresh Start seminars, a nonprofit organization that conducts more than fifty divorce recovery seminars each year for both adults and children throughout the United States. He's a licensed psychologist and the founder and president of Life Counseling Services. Tom has authored or coauthored several books including *The Marriage Mender, Adult AD/HD, Stress Test* (all Piñon Press), and *The Complete Stress Management Workbook* (Zondervan).

We thought he'd be an ideal person to interview about conflict and marriage, because he is a counselor who deals with divorce recovery. Here are his comments.

Toben and Joanne: Do you think the first year of marriage is particularly prone to conflict? Why?

Tom: I'd say that typically the first year of marriage is the most conflict-intense. From the time a couple gets engaged through the first year of their marriage, they are making all kinds of decisions, both big and small. Conflict arises as they work out together how decisions will be made. For example, the wedding itself usually creates a lot of conflict because there are so many decisions to be made. Conflict almost always accompanies times of increased stress.

Toben and Joanne: So decisions are at the heart of most of the conflict during the first year?

Tom: Yes. Most of the conflict that occurs early in a relationship revolves around the power struggle people face. I see less of this happening in mature marriages because these issues get ironed out for most couples early on. Until it gets worked out, marriages can be very conflict-ridden.

Couples have to ask themselves this question: How are our decisions going to be made? And they have to realize that they may not come up with the same answer.

Toben and Joanne: How have you and Lori dealt with the differences in your family backgrounds when it comes to conflict?

Tom: I've seen so much dysfunction in families that I really don't want to be that way. But then something will trigger a reaction.

Maybe my wife says something that sounds just like my mother. When that happens I may overreact because of what that triggers in me. I may get angry. The situation generates fear. If I don't overreact I may instead become more distant. The difficult part is that all of my behavior may be subconscious.

Toben and Joanne: Explain that idea a little more, please.

Tom: Fear typically triggers two responses — fight or flight. I may actively engage a situation that arises and fight for my way. Or I may just say, "Whatever," and walk away. That attitude says, "I'm too important to be bothered by your petty stuff."

Usually people display a combination of behaviors. Some people may have a tendency toward the extremes and they'll always fight or always run. The average person does a little of both.

I have a tendency to let most things go. But every once in a while my masculinity comes into play and I become competitive or angry. I think to myself, "You're not doing that to me, Lori. I'm the man in this family!"

For example, over a period of weeks, I may let a number of

things go that bothered me a little. "When will you be home?" "Who are you talking to?" "Why were you late?" All innocent questions, but perhaps my autonomy is being threatened. Then we progress to questions about our children: "What did you feed them?" "What time did they go to bed?" Again, nothing wrong here, but now I may think my fathering skills are being challenged. Finally, on the way out the door to play football with my son, Lori might suggest, "Don't forget to put a sweater on Kurt!"

Then I snap. "He's fine! Don't you think I know how to dress my son?"

I'm tired of caving in on things, and even though Kurt wearing a sweater wasn't a big deal, it was the thing that finally triggered the "fight" response.

Toben and Joanne: Are there certain issues that typically cause problems in the first year of marriage?

Tom: Every couple has their own trigger issues, especially early in their marriage. Typically those issues are money, sex, children, and the in-laws.

These trigger issues most often provoke the "fight" response whereas smaller issues may produce the "flight" response. Those smaller issues are easier to walk away from but the big ones seem to call for action.

Toben and Joanne: How can we learn what our trigger issues are?

Tom: It's important for couples to analyze what the trigger issues are in their marriage or to identify the topics that are still unsafe. I suggest that couples make an actual list of their trigger issues — money, kids, in-laws, sex, or whatever they may be.

When serious conflict arises and you know that you blew it, analyze what the underlying issue was. Often, regardless of what the fight might at first appear to be about, it comes down to a trigger issue. If you have a blowup and can't find the root of it on your "trigger list" it might be time to add another "trigger" to the list.

The real work begins when you start to make those unsafe trigger issues safe. This happens over a long period of time — sometimes years. Realize that you won't get it all done in your first year of marriage. Identify the easiest one and work through it, and when you get it checked off the list, pick another one and work on it.

Toben and Joanne: What's a trigger issue that you and Lori have dealt with?

Tom: A key issue for Lori and me was money. Lori's mom handles the money in her family, but my dad handles the money in my family. Sometimes I feel threatened when Lori and I have financial issues to deal with. She might ask, "Do we have enough money this month to make a donation to the Right to Life campaign?" If I say, "No, not this week," and Lori asks a reasonable question like "Why?" sometimes I resent it.

I don't want to be questioned about money because I think that Lori is saying, "You're bad at this. Maybe I should manage the finances."

Of course she's not saying that at all. What is the underlying issue? My need or desire to control the money. That's a trigger issue that's been with us for a while, but with lots of work, it now rarely rears its ugly head.

Toben and Joanne: So when conflict arises and a trigger issue surfaces, what's a good way to deal with it?

Tom: After a blowup it's good to set a time to talk about it. And before you get together to discuss what happened, think about what you were feeling.

Then, if you want to, employ what I call the "pencil method." Whoever holds the pencil gets to do the talking. The other person may ask clarifying questions but that's all. Flip a coin and get started. Whoever has the pencil should try only to make feeling statements — "I feel this way when you. . . ." After the person with the pencil has said all he or she has to say, pass the pencil.

Toben and Joanne: Do you think couples should seek counseling for conflict?

Tom: Absolutely. This may sound too simple, but seek counseling when the pencil technique or its equivalent doesn't work. If you're trying to listen to each other but it just isn't working, or if the issue is so hot that you are simply unable to listen to each other, then it's time to get a third-party mediator to help you work through it.

Some couples may think it's a sign of weakness to get that kind of help, but just the opposite is true. It's a sign of strength.

I have couples that come to me for help after fifteen years regarding an issue they have struggled with for every one of those fifteen years. And others come in after a month of marriage. Who do you think is better off?

Toben and Joanne: What are some other issues that can cause conflict early in a marriage?

Tom: Faith can be a trigger issue when one person in the marriage is a Christian and one isn't. Everything revolves around their differences in core beliefs.

The same can be true of Christians who have different views on key issues. Maybe one was raised to be very conservative and the other is more liberal. Specific beliefs can be trigger issues.

Trust is another big issue.

For example, when we were engaged I went to Lori's smelling like smoke from a meeting. Lori asked me, "Were you smoking?" I said no but she wasn't convinced and kept asking.

Lori had dated a guy who often smelled like smoke but had never admitted to being a smoker. After they had gone out for a while, she caught him smoking and knew that he had been lying to her the whole time. It stuck with her.

Usually when we talk about trust early on in marriage we are referring to fidelity, not the smaller stuff like saying one thing but meaning another. Or saying that you will be somewhere at a particular time but always being ten minutes late. Trust is built over time.

Toben and Joanne: What's your best advice for couples just starting out?

Tom: The best advice I can offer is to examine your attitude. That may sound trite, but 80 percent of my arguments are about my attitude: I'm right and she's wrong.

That's the nature of conflict. Force of conviction leads to conflict. If we're not sure about something, that usually leads to communication and then to compromise. When we're sure we are right, we get into fights.

Sacrifice your needs for the sake of your spouse. I usually end up apologizing as I examine my own heart. I think, *What could I have done or said differently?* And the answer usually is, *Check your attitude at the door.*

DISCUSSION QUESTIONS

- How did your family handle conflict?*

- How do you personally react to conflict? Do you clam up, play the victim, or come out swinging? Explain.*

- When you're in conflict with someone, do you want to resolve things fairly (win/win) or do you want to win no matter the cost (zero-sum game)?

- Talk about forgiveness with your partner. Is forgiveness something you're comfortable asking for? Why, or why not?

- Does disagreement equal conflict in your relationship? Explain.*

- What's the worst fight you've had as a couple? What made it so bad?

- Think back to some of the disagreements you've had in the past. What can you learn about each other from them?

- Are there any issues in your relationship that you need to put in the past? What's keeping you from doing so?*

- Are you afraid to disagree? Why, or why not?*

- What rules do you play by in conflict?

- Read Colossians 3:12-14 and Ephesians 4:25-26. Are there any rules for conflict found in these passages that would serve you well?

- Are there any new rules you need to adopt when dealing with conflict? What are they? Would the "Fifteen-Minute Time-Out Rule" or something like it work for you?

_____

* *Questions ideal for journaling*

CHAPTER FOUR

How You Spend

FINANCES

TOBEN:

When Joanne and I were in high school we lived practically next door to each other. Our parents had similar houses and drove similar cars. We shopped at the same stores, went to the same restaurants, and went on similar vacations. Joanne's parents bought her a car, and my parents bought me one too. From all appearances our parents were in the same boat.

The differences in our parents' views of money started to materialize after we went to college. Little by little, it became apparent that my folks were financing their lifestyle while Joanne's folks paid cash for everything. What I witnessed should have taught me a lesson. It didn't.

After we got to college I opened a bank account at a branch down the street from school. They were kind enough to offer me a credit card with a limit about five times greater than my annual income. I didn't really think much about it. For as long as I could remember, that's how my parents paid for things. So I thought that's what people did.

Because of credit, Joanne and I have lived at the same economic level our entire lives. We were middle-class even when we were making next to nothing. We financed our lifestyle at 18- and 21-percent interest. It didn't dawn on us in the early years of our marriage that because we didn't make much money, we shouldn't spend much.

I played golf two or three times a week. We ate out a lot and took a couple of great vacations. We bought a new car and had fantastic wardrobes. And by the time we had been married for a year and a half, we graduated from college with thousands of dollars of credit card debt.

At different times in the years that followed we made significant strides to knock down the debt. We got good jobs after we graduated and started to make a decent living. We continued to pay off our debt but not at the same rate that we continued to pull out that card. Eventually our debt got up to a much higher level than we'd ever expected and hovered there for a couple of years.

I understand, now, very clearly how we got there. I used money to smooth over the rough spots in our relationship. When Joanne and I fought, I would make it up to her by buying her things — clothes, shoes, accessories, you name it. I couldn't figure out how to make things better on my own.

I think my dad took that same route sometimes when I was growing up. I can remember a couple of times when he overwhelmed me with gifts — things so nice I felt a little awkward down deep that he was giving them to me. The first time I remember it happening was when he bought me a bicycle that I really wanted. A couple of years later he bought me another, nicer bicycle. Each one was beautiful and expensive, not from Target or Sears but from a bike shop down the street from our home. He bought me a car for Christmas one year and a better car after my senior year of high school. I got into photography in college and he bought me a lot of equipment, including a couple of great (and expensive) lenses for my camera — which he had bought for me as well.

Please don't misunderstand; I deeply appreciate all he did. His generosity has been overwhelming. But I have a thought in the back of my head that some of what he did was motivated by the fact that things were a little difficult around our house. Suffice it to say, when things got a little rough around the house for Joanne and me, I spent to fix it. Like father, like son.

I also felt compelled to provide for Joanne at the level to which she had been accustomed. Her parents were not exactly thrilled that we had decided to marry so young. They had some valid concerns and a few invalid ones, but the point was that I felt like I needed to earn points with her parents by "taking care" of Joanne.

What turned it around for us? We got pregnant. We had said for years that we wouldn't have a baby until we had a house and were out of debt. God had other plans, because when Joanne came to New York where I was on a business trip and told me the good news, we were still about $15,000 in the hole. After we got over the initial buzz, we got down to business about paying off the debt that had saddled us for so many years.

We Deserve It, Don't We?

JOANNE:

Managing money wasn't new to me. As a young child, I received a dollar each week for allowance. A dime went to church and the rest was for me to save or spend. As I got older and my allowance increased, my dad taught me to keep a notebook recording my allowance income, tithes, expenses, and the few credits I received from babysitting. By the time I opened my first checking account, keeping track of where my money went was second nature.

I wasn't as good at saving my money as my younger sister, Kristen. In the second grade she saved and saved until she had enough money to buy Dallas, Barbie's horse — something I wanted desperately but couldn't afford because I'd spent my allowance on smaller, less exciting purchases. Still, I knew that if I wanted something badly enough I had to save for it . . .

. . . until we got married. I'd had my own VISA for a while — but it was a debit card, not a credit card, so it actually deducted money from my checking account. The VISA we got after we were married was something entirely different. I remember the first time I used it. I was a little nervous as I took it out of my wallet and hesitantly handed it to the cashier. *It's a gift for Toben,* I thought. *Surely that makes it all right.*

Unfortunately, the hesitancy soon vanished as I easily handed it to salespeople over and over again. I felt guilty when the bills arrived and we weren't able to pay the balance. But the guilt disappeared the next time we were out and found something we "just couldn't live without." After all, we deserved it, didn't we?

MONEY, MONEY, MONEY

I have a confession to make: I love ABBA. I first heard their music in the sixth grade and have loved it ever since. As my best friend, Heidi, and I rode in the backseat of her mother's Jetta and sang along with the Swedish supergroup, I decided it would be wonderful to live in "the rich man's world." Money was something I definitely wanted to have — and a lot of it.

As I got older, I realized that chances were slim that my life would end up being full of money. I probably wouldn't live in a mansion with its own elevator like Barbie's or drive a hot-pink convertible. But I did have some specific expectations about money — especially after Toben and I got married.

For one, I expected Toben to be a good money manager. After all, my dad is very smart with money, so why would Toben be any different? To be specific, I expected Toben to balance the checkbook. (And when I say balance, I mean to reconcile it to the bank statement — to the penny.) I never stopped to think how balancing the checkbook would fit in with the fact that Toben has dyslexia — a tendency to switch letters and numbers when he's writing or reading. I also never stopped to ask if he even knew how to balance a checkbook — he didn't.

In fact, Toben just looked at the statement and if he thought the bank's numbers looked right, he filed the statement away in the filing cabinet. In my mind, that was not simply different from how I did it, but totally and utterly wrong.

After talking through my expectations about managing our money, we decided that my expectations weren't very realistic given our personalities, strengths, and weaknesses. So instead, I took over balancing the checkbook — to the penny. Sometimes we have to change our expectations (or even get rid of them altogether) in order to be happy.

My other expectation was that we wouldn't be in so much debt.

DEBT

*T*OBEN:

Here's our best advice about debt: If you're not in debt now, don't get into debt. If you are in debt, don't panic — it's bad, but it's not the end of the world.

Don't panic and think that you are the only ones caught up in debt. The other morning at a Bible study I'm in, one of the guys in the group asked for prayer and encouragement because he and his wife are in debt. Even though they cut up all their cards a year ago, they don't seem to be making any progress. We could all relate to what he was talking about. One by one, about half the guys in the group talked about the debt they had carried (or still carried), ranging from a few thousand dollars to more than $20,000. I was surprised to discover how many of us had walked down that road. I look at these guys and they all seem to be successful, intelligent, ethical people, but they experienced the same failing that I did. I know it was an encouragement to my friend to know that we had all been in his shoes and lived to tell about it. If you start feeling isolated, it might help to talk to someone. Chances are, that person is or has been right where you are.

The emotional impact of debt can be debilitating. I remember losing a lot of sleep. I remember getting up in the middle of the night sometimes to call the credit card companies to check our balance. Then I'd do the math to see whether or not we were going to be able to cover the minimum payments when the bills showed up.

There are two things I wish I'd done. I wish I had talked to Joanne about what was going on. She knew where we stood with our debt, but I don't think she knew how much it was tearing me up inside. I wish I'd let her in so we could have walked through that tough time together.

And I wish we had talked to someone else — an older couple, her parents, or even some of our friends. Sometimes speaking about a fear takes some of the power out of it. The debt wouldn't have disappeared, but letting others in would have given us some accountability, some encouragement, and the prayer support that we desperately needed to get out of debt.

Let me continue by saying that I believe there is such a thing as acceptable debt. Mortgage payments, car payments, or student loan payments are all things that I consider acceptable debt. I know some people will disagree, but I wanted to define a few things before we get into it. As you get ready to talk about all this, a good place to start might be whether or not you buy the idea of "acceptable debt" and, if so, what that might look like.

103

As I mentioned, Joanne and I were in a lot of *un*acceptable debt almost from the beginning of our marriage. We still make a car pay-ment on one of our two cars, and we have a mortgage and student loans, but that's about it. I am not a licensed financial planner or a profes-sional debt counselor, but I can tell you a few things that helped us get out from under our mountain of credit card debt.

Don't send it all to the credit card. At different times, Joanne and I would feel panic-stricken about our debt. We would resolve to send every avail-able penny to the credit card companies to pay down our balances. When the bill arrived, we'd send all the money we could spare. For the first couple of days, that would seem like the good and right thing to do. And then we would need gas for the car, the grocery bill would be a little higher than anticipated, we would want to go out to dinner a couple of times, and I would see some golf thing that I *had* to have. Before we knew it, we were pulling out the credit card again. So we sent the money in to pay off our debt, and all too soon we were spending a second time the money we'd just sent in. Which brings me to our second point.

Set a livable budget and stick to it. Eventually we figured out that if we were going to stick with a budget, it had to be realistic. That meant budgeting for a couple of dinners out, a little more grocery money than we thought we really needed, money for a couple of fill-ups per car, and some spending money to blow on whatever we wanted. Of course, we budgeted to pay back the credit card, and we stuck with that amount — not underpaying or overpaying. If I got a bonus at work, we would send a portion of that money to the credit card but we would set some aside for something fun as well. And we budgeted a portion of our income to savings.

It's important to save. It is hard to send money to savings when you're trying to get out of debt, but we didn't want to end up falling back on the credit card for emergencies like car repairs. We set up a savings plan that withdrew a certain amount from our paychecks every month — we never even saw it. It went into an account that earned a good interest rate and provided a cushion for us to fall back on. So when our beagle Daisy had an allergic reaction to some antibiotics and (don't laugh) needed to have a blood transfusion (she's now part Doberman), which resulted in a stay at the veterinarian's for nearly a week, we were able to handle it.

Don't forget to give. If you think putting money into savings is hard when you're trying to get out from under credit card debt, try putting money in the offering plate at church every week.

I have a friend named Steve. For a time, we got together once a week to hold each other accountable in our lives. One of my primary struggles was this whole debt thing. I remember Steve asking, "Why don't you pray and ask God to help you get out of debt and trust Him for that help?" My immediate response was "I got myself into this and I'll get myself out of it, thank you very much." But deeper than that was a sense of shame that I carried around about it. And like it is with most shame, I didn't want to share it with God — even though He already knew it all. After a little while, I began asking God for help.

As we listened for God's counsel in this area of our lives, we began to see that our money really isn't our money at all — it belongs to God. So we decided to demonstrate that by giving a portion of our income back to Him. We decided that 10 percent was a good place to start. When paychecks arrived, the first check we wrote went to our church or a Christian organization that we'd decided to support. Things immediately turned around. Our debt didn't magically disappear, but God provided us with the money we needed to pay back what we owed through things like bonuses at work and unexpected refunds from everything from insurance to magazine subscriptions.

First Steps

Do you have a budget? Do you stick to it?

Hanna: Yes.

Brian: We do?

Hanna: Yes, but we don't really stick to it!

BUDGETING

I've mentioned budgeting a few times already but I want to address it more specifically. Trying to figure out your financial life without a budget is like . . . well, it's really difficult. Thankfully, there are many different ways to budget, and you're sure to eventually find a system that clicks for you.

Joanne and I did one thing early on that got us over a lot of financial humps. We both worked, and for the most part, we kept our finances separate. Joanne and I each had a checking account, and we divided up the budgetary responsibilities. Joanne paid one of the car payments and I made the payment on the other. I paid the rent and she paid the insurance, and so on. After we covered our responsibilities, whatever was left over was ours to spend on what we wanted.

This was a great arrangement for us because Joanne and I have very different interests and spending habits. Joanne loves decorating and all things crafty. She typically spends quite a bit of her discretionary money at Hobby Lobby. I can't stand that place.

Almost all of my discretionary spending goes to golf or some golf-related thing. Joanne can't figure out what difference one driver or putter makes from another, so my spending often looks ridiculous to her. Because our finances were separate, these spending habits were never a big deal. One rule: When either one of us ran out of spending money, we were out until payday.

We took turns paying for dinners out or movie tickets. There was never a rigidity about it and it worked great. Now that Joanne is no longer earning a paycheck, we have budgeted an amount that she gets in cash at the beginning of every pay period, but the concept is the same. She has some responsibilities to cover with that money, and whatever is left over is hers.

We have some friends who have used an envelope system pretty successfully. In fact, that's how we started budgeting while we were in college and didn't have any money. Joanne's parents gave us a bunch of envelopes labeled with specific categories and filled with cash to get us started. At the beginning of each pay period you put cash in the envelopes — eating out, groceries, clothes, gas, and so on. When an envelope is empty, that's it. (Unfortunately, we turned to VISA when the envelope emptied too quickly.) By the way, it's often the "little things" or incidentals that are the budget culprits. Take a month or two to record everything you spend. You'll be surprised how quickly cups of coffee, fast food, and other small items add up.

Our friends share the money in each of those envelopes. That means if one of them wants a new pair of shoes (and they both have great taste in shoes) he or she may have to negotiate to get the entire clothing budget for that month. Maybe that means the spouse gets it all the month after. Joanne and I also got into the habit of printing our budget from our computer and putting it on the fridge (another couple we knows keeps theirs in the front of the filing cabinet). We would fold it in half so company couldn't see all the gory details, but having it up there was a good and constant reminder of what we were doing. We would even make empty boxes beside each line item so we could check things off as we took care of them each month. This helped ensure that everything got covered before we hit the spending money.

Budgeting is a very personal activity, and you'll have to figure out what works best for you in your situation. Whatever your approach, budgeting can be a great opportunity to talk about spending habits, saving habits, giving habits, and financial expectations. Take advantage of it. Not talking about it will get you in trouble every time. And remember, once you have a budget, review it from time to time to make sure that you are sticking with it and that it's still working.

GIVING

I've mentioned giving a couple of times and want to share something that has been significant for Joanne and me. We love our church and we love to give to our church, but occasionally we will give some of that money, as anonymously as possible, to someone in need. There is little that is as rewarding as being able to help someone out of a jam. We learned something about that from a group of friends.

I'd been in the hospital for a month as a result of a couple of intestinal surgeries. No big deal, right? But two surgeries and a month in the hospital added up to about $110,000. We had pretty good insurance through work, but our share of that bill came to about $3,000. We figured we would have to add that to our debt and pay it off over time. One Sunday after church, while I was still at home recovering, Steve and Andrea came by the house and gave us a check that covered a third of that amount. Joanne and I were both speechless. Steve and Andrea and a bunch of other couples from our Sunday school class had pitched in to help out. And the financial help wasn't the end of it. They provided meals and support that meant everything to us at the time.

We've used their example in our own giving. While we usually decide at the beginning of the year the organizations we'll support with our tithe money, these friends taught us to be flexible. Just this past week we were invited to a baby shower for a teenage mom we've never met. She just moved here and the baby is due in a couple of weeks. She needed everything — from furniture to bedding to baby books. We decided to take our tithe money (and then some!) and get her a bunch of stuff she needed. It was so much fun to go all out in getting her the crib bedding, nursery decorations, and toys she really wanted for her new baby. But the real fun was seeing the expression on her face and knowing that we were helping to meet a need.

Perhaps our experience or one of your own will spur you as a couple to keep your eyes open for people around you who need help. No matter how tight things may be, there is always someone nearby who is in worse shape than you are.

First Steps

Do you tithe?

Brian: Yes, we do — mostly to the church we attend. I saw the habit of tithing in my parents as a child, but they didn't really model it to me in terms of what it was and why they did it.

Hanna: My parents weren't Christians until I was in high school. Mom and Dad did a lot of reading about tithing and talked to us kids about it. They talked about the fact that it wasn't our money and that you could really test God in tithing. If you gave money to Him, He would honor it. We tithe because I believe we should and because I believe things would be worse financially if we weren't tithing.

IN SUMMARY

As in every other aspect of marriage, communication is key to getting your financial act together. If you don't talk about it, things will surely go wrong. A couple who were about to be married asked us, "How do you guys make your money situation work? You keep your finances separate, but Toben makes more money than Joanne does. How do you keep it fair?"

The answer was simple: We talk about it. We love each other and want what is best for one another, so we communicate, compromise, evaluate, and reevaluate everything we do. If something doesn't work, we change it. And if it does work, we try to make it even better.

The critical elements are these: Take a realistic view of your finances, come up with a plan (a budget or a strategy to get out of debt, for example), don't forget to save, and don't forget to give. Don't be afraid to ask for advice and don't let yourselves feel isolated. Get the support and accountability you need. If necessary, find a financial mentor, perhaps even a trusted older couple. The benefit will definitely outweigh some of the initial discomfort at disclosing the contents of your checkbook.

∽

VOICE OF WISDOM

When Chuck and Kay Friedenstein got married on December 20, 1968, gasoline cost $.30 per gallon, their rent was $75 a month, and they could buy groceries for two for only $25 a week. It makes money and a new marriage sound a lot easier than it is now. (Of course, minimum wage was only $1.25 or so per hour at that time too!) Though prices have gone up a lot since they were first married, they had to learn to manage their money wisely then, just as couples do today.

As they talk about their own families and how their parents handled money, they're quick to agree that their families were very similar. "Our parents grew up during the Depression," Chuck says. "As a result, they were very conservative and careful with their money." Kay recalls that her family rarely went out to eat, save the occasional meal after church on Sunday at a buffet restaurant.

As they describe their family backgrounds, Chuck laughs as he recalls his own father. "I can remember my father standing over me and shaking his finger. 'You don't know the value of a dollar,' he'd say." Kay adds, "Don't forget this one: 'Don't spend what you don't have!'"

Even though they laugh about the financial advice they received from their parents, the advice stuck. "All four of our parents worked for the government as civil servants on an hourly wage," Chuck says. "But through hard work and a conservative view of money, they all managed to save a lot of money. That has kept me going through the years as I've looked back on their example."

But like most couples, they did make money mistakes. "In the time after we were first married, I had these unrealistic visions of wealth," Chuck says. "Some of the guys in my office were trying to beat the stock market. They were making money from it, so I joined in with money from our savings. To make a long story short, I lost about $1,500 — which was a lot for us."

"I remember Chuck coming home each day sick with worry," Kay says. "It was scary to know we could lose money so easily."

"I had just become a Christian," Chuck says, "and it seemed to me that God was telling me to lay aside my desire for wealth and to replace it with a desire for Him instead. After we lost the money, I became much more conservative financially — and I still am conservative when it comes to money."

As they talked about starting out, it became evident that one of the big differences in their experience and the experiences of young couples today is credit. In 1968, VISA, MasterCard, Discover, American Express, and all the rest weren't quite so prevalent. "The main credit cards people we knew had were from a particular department store or gas station," Chuck recalls. "If you didn't have the money, you didn't have the money."

"We budgeted using envelopes," Kay says. "And when the envelope was empty, it was empty. There was no credit card to fall back on."

Budgeting played a big role in Chuck and Kay's early marriage. Because Chuck still had one semester of college to finish before moving to California and joining the Air Force, they didn't have an income and instead lived off their savings for the first six months. The grand total? A little over $1,000. They decided to keep about a third of their savings in the bank as a cushion. Each week, they filled their labeled envelopes with cash — $25 for groceries, a quarter for each wash load and a dime for the dryer, a certain amount for their church, and $2 for spending.

So, what did they spend their spending money on? "Every Sunday night, we drove to this local restaurant and had a spaghetti dinner," Kay says. "Spaghetti, salad, garlic bread, and a drink — all for $1. It was a bargain, even then."

Other differences between their experience and the experiences of couples today? "Car payments," says Chuck. "So many people today feel like they have to have a new car — or two." Another difference that comes up is eating out. It seems like so many people eat out frequently — and that quickly adds up to a big expense. "You could buy groceries for a week for what it costs to eat out at some restaurants," Kay remarks.

Chuck and Kay talk about money in terms of what they need and what they can afford, while so many people today talk in terms of what they want and what they can finance. It's a whole different mindset.

So what advice about managing money would they offer young couples?

"I think the smartest thing we've done with money is never borrowing for anything other than a house," says Chuck. And even that took a lot of saving. "After we moved to Los Angeles and both started working, we lived on one salary and banked the other," Kay says. "We each only made about $300 a month, but we knew we wanted a house and a family. We planned for me to stay home when we had children, so we decided to learn to live on one salary early on."

"The other advice I would offer about money is this," Chuck adds. "Pay God, pay yourself by saving, and then budget the rest — in that order."

Things have changed a lot since 1968, but being smart with money never changes, no matter what things cost. Even in the first century, people struggled with money. The apostle Paul wrote this to Timothy:

114

> But godliness with contentment is great gain. For we brought nothing into the world, and we can take nothing out of it. But if we have food and clothing, we will be content with that. People who want to get rich fall into temptation and a trap and into many foolish and harmful desires that plunge men into ruin and destruction. For the love of money is a root of all kinds of evil. Some people, eager for money, have wandered from the faith and pierced themselves with many griefs (1 Timothy 6:6-10, NIV).

"Godliness with contentment is great gain," quotes Chuck. "That's the key. We need to learn to be content with what we have."

Discussion Questions

- How did your family view money, particularly debt?*

- If you think your spouse's family viewed money and debt differently, where do you see potential challenges due to those differences?*

- Do you have debt? How do you feel about it?

- How do you feel about borrowing money? From the bank? From friends? From family?

- What do you think about living on one salary and saving the other? Is that something you could do? Why, or why not?

- Would you rather spend less and get something cheap or spend more for quality? Why?

- When you get a paycheck, do you spend it quickly, or does it last until the next paycheck?

- If money were no object, what would you buy?*

- Describe your views on saving money.

- Do you both plan to work? Would that change if you had children? How?

- What are your expectations about how you will handle your money as a couple?*

- Do you have a budget? Do you stick to it?

- Do you plan on having joint bank accounts or separate accounts? Why?

- If you have debt, do you have a realistic plan to get out of it?

- Do you tithe? If not, do you think you should start?

- What churches or ministries would you like to support with your tithe?

- What are your personal financial goals? What about your goals as a couple?*

Questions ideal for journaling

CHAPTER FIVE

What You Expect

S E X

JOANNE:

Call me old-fashioned, but I was a virgin when we got married. Growing up in a conservative Christian home, I was pretty convinced that having sex before I got married was the ultimate in unforgivable sins.

But after watching several daughters from the handful of pastors at church get pregnant and then quickly get married, I decided that sex before marriage wasn't the worst thing I could do — despite the subtle (and not so subtle!) messages coming from my parents.

Don't get me wrong — sex sure sounded great. And none (well, almost none) of the people doing it in the romance novels I read were married. True, these books were fiction, but I didn't realize just how fictional they were until our wedding night. I expected our clothes to fall off on their own — not the painstakingly slow process of undoing the millions of buttons down the back of my wedding dress. I expected my hair to fall in luxurious waves when I took it down from my veil — not the itch caused by the birdseed that was stuck in it, which I had to harshly comb out with my head upside down over the bathtub. I expected heaving bosoms, waves of ecstasy, and sex straight out of a Harlequin romance novel.

HEAVING BOSOMS AND WAVES OF ECSTASY

We lived across the street from the library when I was in the sixth grade. The library was small, but well stocked with teen romances. I read *P.S. I Love You,* and I was hooked. I checked out those books six or seven at a time, read them late at night, and hid them under my bed during the day.

My heart raced to read about the popular boy and the shy girl who fell in love across the science lab. I hurried through the pages of the budding romance to their first kiss and dreamed of falling in love someday and finding someone who would make my palms sweat and my heart pound.

From teen romances filled with first kisses, I moved on to adult romances. Fashionably dressed women met dashing and dangerous men who made love to them with reckless abandon — all with a lot of detail. Here were the heaving bosoms, the waves of ecstasy, and passion beyond measure.

Needless to say, sex didn't turn out to be what I expected. How could it? I'd built up a fantasy in my mind, never bothered to tell Toben what I was expecting, and forgot to take into account the fact that I'd never done it before and that trying anything for the first time can be difficult.

When I asked my friend Kathy if sex was what she expected, the answer was quick and forceful. "No! Romance novels take way too many liberties." So do the movies.

"When my husband and I were dating, I really felt the passion that movies and romances portray," said another friend. "We had such chemistry that we both thought sex would be this incredible, never-ending passionate drive. I could see us having sex like they do in the movies once we were married. My ideals were really high. I now think that sex portrayed in the movies is a huge lie. It paints this picture of sex that isn't even the slightest bit accurate, and then we're disappointed."

After all, sex in the movies is always spontaneous, always romantic, and always clean. When Toben and I were engaged, I remember an older woman describing how messy sex is. *Gross,* I thought. *It can't really be like that. She must be wrong.* And I went on thinking that sex was the fantasy I'd built it up to be.

As a woman, I think that my greatest expectation was that sex — or maybe more accurately that Toben — would always be romantic. Soft music, flowers, candlelight — I wanted it all.

119

First Steps

Where did your expectations of sex come from?

Hanna: My parents. They have always had a really active, wonderful sex life. My dad told me once that you don't have good sex until ten years after you're married. So I never expected it to be great right away. I knew that sex takes learning and that the more we got to know one another, the better it would get. But even though I know it in my head, it's still hard when it's not easy or great.

Brian: Porn. I was exposed to pornography at an early age. It really influenced my thoughts on sex. I grew up in a neighborhood that was terrific. We lived right next to a park with tons of kids roughly my age. But for the most part, my friends were four to six years older than me. That was sometimes good, but it meant that I was exposed to things ahead of the curve. My expectations of sex were that it would be fantastic because that's how porn presented it. We're both working it out because my expectations were so high.

FUMBLING TOWARD ECSTASY — OR SOMETHING LIKE THAT

TOBEN:

I didn't know what to expect from sex when Joanne and I got married.

120   I hadn't read any romance novels. I hadn't seen a *Playboy* magazine or watched porno movies. Joanne made me watch *Days of Our Lives* with her a few times when we were dating and that gave me a few ideas, but that was about it. I'd had sex before Joanne and I met (I'll talk about that more a little later), but it was largely loveless and fumbling and didn't translate into what I expected for Joanne and me.

I'd do over two things related to romance and sex if I could. The first is the way Joanne and I became engaged. We had Romeo and Juliet syndrome big time. We felt like her folks would never accept our relationship and feared they were seeking to drive us apart. Out of desperation more than anything else, we decided to get engaged. I bought a ring, we left her parents a note telling them what we were about to do, and then we went to a favorite spot where I proposed. That experience eliminated any surprise and was full of fear because we knew we'd have to see her parents later that night — and that they were going to be unhappy.

What I wouldn't give to have an opportunity to "pop the question" as a surprise to Joanne, feeling nothing but the joy and expectancy of the moment. But there really isn't a do-over for this one. The other do-over I would take is the first time Joanne and I had sex.

That sounds terrible as I read it back to myself, but let me explain. As we mentioned earlier, we were dead tired and covered in birdseed when we arrived at our hotel the night of our wedding. It was well past midnight, and we could hardly keep our eyes open. I wanted Joanne so badly that when we fell into bed, I went at it like she was a meal for a starving man. I didn't have a thought in my head about what might make her feel good or special or cared for. I think we'd read a few books for couples about to be married that included a few diagrams and descriptions of how to have sex the "right way." Apparently they didn't have much of an impact. I know I am not the first guy in history to be selfish in bed, but boy, oh boy, was I ever.

If I could have that do-over I would do one thing differently — I would think. I would take a moment to breathe. Sex includes so much more than biology. That's the thing that didn't dawn on me for some time. Even now on occasion I get wrongheaded about what makes sex work. I get that "starving man" syndrome all over again without thinking about the fact that Joanne is an emotional and spiritual being as well as a physical one. Realizing that would have made the first time very different.

BEYOND ALL EXPECTATIONS

*J*OANNE:

What I didn't expect from sex was the mystery of it. From our first attempt at making love, there was something amazing happening beyond our nervousness and lack of skill. As close as we were and as much as we loved each other already, sex bonded us in a way nothing else did — or could.

In 1 Corinthians, Paul says, "There's more to sex than mere skin on skin. Sex is as much spiritual mystery as physical fact. As written in Scripture, 'The two become one'" (6:16). I understood the mechanics of sex but not much more. I knew in my head that "the two become one," but I didn't understand how profound and how true that really is. For the first time, I really understood why God intends sex to be held within marriage. Paul goes on to say, "Sexual drives are strong, but marriage is strong enough to contain them and provide for a balanced and fulfilling sexual life in a world of sexual disorder" (7:2).

LIKE A VIRGIN

I said earlier that I was a virgin when we got married. And I was — technically. But though I'd never had intercourse, I had fooled around plenty. I'm a little embarrassed to tell this story, but here goes.

I'm happy to say that the majority of the making out I did before I got married was with Toben. I struggled for years with guilt over it and can't imagine how much worse it would be if it had been with someone other than Toben. Nowhere in the Bible is there a line defining just what's acceptable and what's not. I'd always thought that was up to me. I think differently now. Before I go on, let me say to those of you who are engaged that I don't want to tell you what's appropriate for you sexually before marriage. I do want to say that your attitude is of vital importance.

I was reading my Bible the other morning and came across a verse that made me stop: "Just because something is technically legal doesn't mean that it's spiritually appropriate. If I went around doing whatever I thought I could get by with, I'd be a slave to my whims" (I Corinthians 6:12). Ouch! That verse describes exactly how I viewed our physical relationship before we got married. Instead of thinking about what was spiritually appropriate, I was caught up in the technicality of it all — what I could get by with.

The good news is that God has something better in mind. When our attitude is one of wanting what's spiritually appropriate, God grants us a new freedom. Paul talks more about this in Romans 7:5-6:

> For as long as we lived that old way of life, doing whatever we felt we could get away with, sin was calling most of the shots as the old law code hemmed us in. And this made us all the more rebellious. In the end, all we had to show for it was miscarriages and stillbirths. But now that we're no longer shackled to that domineering mate of sin, and out from under all those oppressive regulations and fine print, we're free to live a new life in the freedom of God.

This freedom is not one to do whatever we please, but a freedom that comes from doing what's right. As I've come to terms with my sexual past and asked God to forgive me, I've discovered a new freedom that I've not felt before — freedom from past guilt and freedom in our sexual relationship after marriage.

UNLIKE A VIRGIN

*T*OBEN:

Let me first say that I hate writing about this. I am embarrassed to this day of the fact that I was sexually active before Joanne and I met. No longer ashamed or filled with regret, but certainly embarrassed.

My high school girlfriend and I slept together a few times. To most folks, especially nonChristian folks, that may not seem like a big deal. And to a lot of Christians it won't seem like a big deal either. I've always heard that rates of premarital sexuality among Christians and nonChristians are roughly equivalent — and based on conversations I've had with Christian friends, I'd guess that's correct. But believe me when I tell you that as soon as I got serious about Joanne, it was a very big deal to me.

Sometimes I think that if she had slept around a little I wouldn't have felt so bad, but she hadn't. What to do? How do we get over the fact that even before I knew Joanne I had done something that was going to have such an impact on our relationship?

One thing I knew from the beginning was that Joanne felt terrible about what I had done too. And she had a right to. She had delayed gratification so that when she found the man she was going to marry, she could enter into that relationship with a clean slate and a clear conscience.

Early on we decided that whenever she felt sad or angry because of what I had done, she could bring it up. See, a sexual relationship is a tricky one for most of us. It is an incredibly joyful and vulnerable thing. Bringing baggage to bed can mess things up quickly.

For us, the quickest and most direct way to check that baggage was to be honest. When Joanne felt resentment and hurt bubbling up, she would bring it up and we would talk it through. This runs counter to one of my primary communication beliefs: that once something is settled, the past stays in the past. But with this issue, especially, the past has a way of coming back again and again. So that's what we did.

It hasn't come up for some time now, but if it ever comes up again, that's okay with me. I did the crime and I'll do the time. If what I did gets in the way of who Joanne and I are intended to be as husband and wife, then we can talk about it anytime she feels the need. This is really only true because I trust Joanne not to bring it up out of spite or because she wants to punish me. It's perfectly okay if she needs to be reassured that, regardless of the past, she is my wife and I love her more dearly than I love myself (and I tend to love myself quite a bit). 125

THE TWO BECOME ONE

JOANNE:

"You may kiss the bride." Five little words that to me seemed to be a license to do what we'd wanted and waited to do for so long — have sex! What was once taboo, forbidden, and totally against the rules was suddenly ours for the taking. We were thrilled!

At the same time, it was difficult for me to understand how something that had always been "bad" was now "good." It was strange to arrive at Toben's parents' house for brunch the morning after the wedding knowing that everyone knew — and approved — that we'd had sex the night before. Especially when just a week ago, they would have been furious and I would have been grounded until I was forty-five.

While being modest — dare I say "prudish" — is often presented as an admirable quality in virginal girls, I slowly learned that such modesty has no place in marriage. None. What was once entirely appropriate — keeping the goods to myself, as it were — is no longer acceptable. In fact, we're commanded to have sex regularly.

> *Abstaining from sex is permissible for a period of time if you both agree to it, and if it's for the purposes of prayer and fasting — but only for such times. Then come back together again. Satan has an ingenious way of tempting us when we least expect it. I'm not, understand, commanding these periods of abstinence — only providing my best counsel if you should choose them (1 Corinthians 7:5-6).*

Great sex in marriage is something that God wants us to experience — and often. *No problem,* you think. But that's one expectation that doesn't always get met.

"When we got married, I expected we'd be logging a lot of time in bed," Kathy told me. "I guess I expected it because of the way that everyone jokes about newlyweds."

"I thought we'd be passionate all the time," another friend said.

One of Toben's friends said that sex every day just isn't realistic — especially when kids come along. (And now, as parents, we know just how right he was!) Finding time and space for you as a couple becomes difficult when you're working around naps — your own and the baby's.

It's pretty obvious that great sex doesn't come naturally. It's a learned art. So practice, practice, practice. (Is it any wonder that the Song of Songs is included in the group of Old Testament books called the Wisdom books?) So what does it take to have great sex?

TALK DIRTY TO ME

Despite the fact that Toben knows me better than anyone else, has seen me naked countless times, and loves me no matter what, I'd rather talk with him about anything other than sex. Some counselors have said that sex is typically the most difficult subject for a couple to discuss. I believe it.

I have no trouble reading about it — for a time, the more sex a romance novel had, the better it was as far as I was concerned. I don't even have a hard time imagining what I want to say. The words describing my wants, my fears, and my feelings come easily until I open my mouth. But once it's time to speak the words aloud, I become embarrassed, self-conscious, and tongue-tied. All of which leave me feeling ridiculous, more embarrassed, and even angry. Not a good combination to say the least.

I shouldn't have to tell him this, I think. *If he loves me, he'll know how I feel, what I want, what feels good and bad.* And therein lies the problem. I have expectations that I don't voice. When those naturally go unmet (How can he meet them if he doesn't even know about them?), it leaves me feeling upset, sad, hurt — whatever. And, in my mind anyway, it's all his fault. Not very fair, is it?

For some reason, it seems perfectly fair until I see it here on the computer screen. *Am I really like that?* I ask myself. Yep. Unfortunately, I'm not the only one who feels that way. In her book, Kathy Miller tells about a young woman who approached her at a women's retreat:

> *Leslie is typical of the many women I listen to during private counseling sessions when I speak at women's retreats. "I so much want Jeff to arrange*

127

romantic times," she told me, as tears dribbled down her cheeks. "I daydream about walking on the beach with him or having a picnic at our local park."

Gently I inquired, "Have you told Jeff what you want?"

Leslie looked at me with surprise. "Oh, no. If I have to tell him what to do, it doesn't have as much meaning. Then I'd feel like I'd forced him to do it."

For a long time, I felt the same way. But this perspective is a corollary to the myth that our husbands can read our minds.

Judy, a woman who has learned to express her romantic needs, gives us a better outlook. "I realize that my husband appreciates my romantic suggestions. It's not that he doesn't want to meet my needs; he simply doesn't think about it. I can value what he does for me because he chooses to do it and it requires his energy."[1]

128

I can't stress it enough: Whether they're realistic or not, you have to look at what your expectations about sex are and where they come from. And, no matter how tough it is, you have to talk about them before they can even begin to be met.

Maybe talking about sex is easier for you than it is for me. Maybe it's more difficult for you. I certainly don't have it all figured out yet. In fact, I'm hesitant to admit that after being married twelve years, I'm still terrible at this and haven't given it as much effort as I've given to learning to make the perfect chocolate cake.

Commit to talking with your spouse about your sex life — about the wedding night and beyond. Be accountable with your spouse about your feelings surrounding sex. Decide together to pay attention to your communication about sex and set healthy, open patterns early in your marriage.

FIRST STEPS

How comfortable are you talking about sex with your partner?

Hanna: I think we're fairly comfortable, but Brian's more comfortable than I am. He's far more comfortable with his body than I am with mine. He asks me a lot of questions. If we didn't talk about it, I'd be very depressed. If I didn't know his heart, I could be very hurt. But he tells me that he's trying and that he wants to make sex as good as it can be.

Brian: I'm absolutely comfortable talking about sex. I don't know where that came from.

Hanna: Did it come from your high school Bible study?

Brian: It could have. I think it was more about the fact that from the time I was a freshman in high school, I was surrounded by people who were comfortable talking about just about anything. I don't think it came from my family though. In sixth-grade sex ed class, we had to choose a question to ask each of our parents. I remember it being awkward to talk with both of my parents. I just remember feeling like I should apologize for subjecting them to the assignment.

HIS NEEDS, HER NEEDS

So where do you begin when you start talking about sex? Try your expectations. Do you expect sex to be planned or spontaneous? Do you expect your spouse to initiate sex, or do you feel comfortable making the first move? Do you expect to have sex every day or once a week? Is it okay to say you're just not in the mood?

Some of our friends who have been married almost four years talked a lot about sex before they were married. "We talked to a lot of people about what sex is like," Rebecca told me. "We knew that we wouldn't have a hot love scene the first time, and we communicated about it a lot. On our wedding night, neither of us was disappointed."

If you're new at sex, try talking about what feels good and what doesn't. It's okay to say what you like. While the purpose of this book is not to explain sex or dictate what a good sex life looks like, we think it's a good idea to take a look at the whole idea of needs. There are a lot of books available with specific information on sex (see the "Resources" section for some starters). Consider reading a good book about sex together — maybe even aloud — and discuss what you learn.

Needs in and of themselves are pretty value-neutral as far as I'm concerned — neither good nor bad. But I think there is a danger surrounding the whole issue of needs as they relate to sex. As humans, we tend to be a pretty selfish bunch — and getting married doesn't change that a bit. (In fact, marriage seems to have a way of accentuating my selfishness!) And when we focus too much on our needs, we get selfish and "stand up for our rights" instead of deciding to meet our spouse's needs.

Paul communicates this idea clearly in his letter to the Corinthians: "The marriage bed must be a place of mutuality — the husband seeking to satisfy his wife, the wife seeking to satisfy her husband. Marriage is not a place to 'stand up for your rights.' Marriage is a decision to serve the other, whether in bed or out" (1 Corinthians 7:3-4).

Sex isn't an exception when it comes to how you relate to your spouse. Every part of marriage is an opportunity to serve each other, putting the other's needs before your own. All too often, I find myself standing up for my rights rather than focusing on Toben and his needs. At the end of the day, I often think about what I need from him when he comes home rather than thinking of how I can help him relax after a tough day at work. Satisfying my husband requires a change in my thinking, as I choose to think of someone else's needs before thinking of my own.

A single friend once told me that she has never really wanted to get married. "I just don't see marriage as something positive," she said. "Most of the time it looks pretty miserable." Then she paid me the nicest compliment I've ever received: "But when I see you and Toben together, I think, *Maybe I would like to get married someday. They make it look like so much fun.*"

Don't get me wrong. Toben and I don't have the perfect marriage. There's a lot of room for improvement here and there. But it makes me excited to think about the possibilities and the potential our marriage — not just our sex life — has if we consistently work to serve the other instead of standing up for ourselves. What a witness Christian couples could have if they followed this basic biblical principle and modeled marriages that stand out in our world, giving others a positive picture of what marriage can be like!

IN SUMMARY

More than any other aspect of marriage, it seems like sex is one where we have expectations that we don't communicate and, as a result, that don't get met. And, more than other aspects of marriage, sex is hard to talk about for many couples.

The good news is that God wants us to have great sex with our spouses. One of the reasons God created sex was for pleasure. As you examine your expectations about sex and talk them through with your partner, you'll discover greater intimacy. Take your time. Great sex doesn't come right away. You have your whole lives to have sex with each other — you don't have to get it perfect the first time.

And remember, the sexiest part of the body is the brain. Think, talk, and use your imagination!

∞

VOICE OF WISDOM

Jack and Carole Mayhall work with The Navigators in Colorado Springs, Colorado. Both of them speak frequently at conferences and seminars around the country. Carole is the author of *Words That Hurt, Words That Heal* and *When God Whispers* (both NavPress).

The following is excerpted from *Marriage Takes More Than Love*, based on a marriage seminar the Mayhalls have presented worldwide.

Choosing to understand sexual differences (by Jack)

Sexually, men and women are different. And anatomy is only a small part of that difference. We are diverse in our approaches, our responses, and what sex means to us. Unless we understand and adjust to these variances, we are in trouble.

Now, what I have written may not apply to everyone, but here are some distinctives:

- To a man sex is a delightful intermission in the drama; to a woman it is inexorably woven into the fabric of the whole.
- The male sex drive is generated by physical needs, accompanied by emotional needs; a woman's drive stems from emotional needs, along with physical needs.
- A man thinks, *How often?* A woman ponders, *How?*
- A man's thought is reduced to the moment; a woman's to what is produced by the moment. (During intercourse, a man rarely thinks of the act resulting in a baby, while this may be much on a woman's mind.)

- A man is quick to react to stimulation; a woman, comparatively slow to react, needs to be stimulated.
- A man is primarily stimulated by one of his senses — sight; a woman is stimulated by all five plus one — touch, hearing, sight, taste, and smell. The extra "plus one" is tenderness. (This difference is important. A number of wives have confided to Carole and me that they were unable to respond physically to their husbands because they smelled. Perspiration, stale smoke, and bad breath can all inhibit a woman's enjoyment of sex. It is also true that men can be turned off by unpleasant smells, but women seem to be more sensitive to such things.)

134

To summarize with an illustration: A man is like an electric light bulb — you flip a switch and on he goes. A woman is more like an electric iron — you flip a switch and it takes a little time to warm up. When you turn it off, it takes a bit of time to cool off too. Now, if you don't remember any of the other differences, please remember that one. It is very important in learning to be a lover. And men need to learn to be lovers if they are to satisfy the needs of their wives.

I get discouraged sometimes when I talk with some men about their pattern in making love. Some have the lovemaking instincts of a frog, and maybe I'm being disrespectful to a frog!

Note this often-typical situation. He gets home from work and gives her a little peck on the cheek. They have supper. He sits down and relaxes, reads the paper, and watches some television. Then it is bedtime. So he goes into the bathroom, does his little chores, and gets into his pajamas. She does the same thing, and they climb into bed. They read a little while, perhaps, and then she reaches over and turns off her light. He reads a few minutes longer and finally reaches over and turns off his light. All is quiet.

And then, suddenly, out of the dark . . . comes a hand.

What a romantic setting! What psychological buildup! What creative imagination! Like I said, "All the instincts of a frog!"

Now, men, we can do better than that.

One time, a month after we had presented this subject to a group at a seminar, I ran into one of the women who had attended. She smiled and said, "You know, now my husband on occasion will call in the afternoon from the office and as we are chatting will say, 'By the way, honey, will you please turn on the iron?'"

She was excited about that.

If a man has on his mind all day a desire to make love that evening and is just waiting to get home that night, but his wife doesn't know anything about it, if she can respond with enthusiasm when he pulls that "hand in the dark" routine, then he has a very unusual wife.

On the other hand, if, as he leaves the house in the morning, he gives her a very warm kiss and communicates in their own secret little code that he is looking forward to some fun that night, it will turn up her thermostat just a bit and it will stay warm all day long. By the time he gets home, the atmosphere has already been created and the two are far more likely to have a wonderful time that night.

We are all unique individuals. So talk together about your needs and ideas to promote greater mutual enjoyment in your sex lives. If you want "an angel in the home and a tigress in bed," you

135

must communicate what excites and pleasures you.

Have you ever discussed the degree of dress or undress that stimulates desire? Or the kind of apparel? Some men who don't like black nightgowns have not said so, and their wives have been buying black nightgowns for years with the mistaken notion that their husbands found them sexy.

Those of us who have been married some years hopefully have gotten courageous enough to walk into the lingerie department of a large store and bravely walk up to the counter (as though we do it every day of the week) and say, "I'll take one of those." The "those" is something that she will wear only for you, a gesture of love and appreciation, but also something that will excite you.

May God deliver us from the "hand in the dark" approach. We need to use our imaginations and our creativity to set the mood for our lovemaking. Sex should be fun. And variety will enhance that fun.

Have you ever used your imagination to create a whole other world for your lovemaking? Your imagination can transport you out of that bedroom and the monotony of its four walls so that you can journey together to a desert island where you are marooned with no rescue in sight, or to a little cabin, snowbound after skiing all day. Imagining wholesome situations, different times, diverse places all can add to your enjoyment together.

Good ideas can also be obtained from many marriage manuals, but many couples read the wrong ones or too many of them. They get so wrapped up in the "ideal" that they become totally unreal. Many manuals, for instance, hold that the epitome of the sex relationship is to have a climax together. This can be like a carrot held out to a bunch of racing rabbits — always just out of reach. As long as both are enjoying the physical relationship and both are usually reaching a climax, it just isn't that important to reach it together. The enjoyment is the primary concern. And the climax will not be the same every time. I have talked to people who are disappointed unless they have the greatest, most exciting feeling in their lives each time. It is always exciting — or should be. It is always thrilling, but it is never the same.

One of my favorite meals is a steak, a baked potato, rolls, and apple pie. That is a real banquet for me. But I also like McDonald's hamburgers. In fact, I'm crazy about McDonald's hamburgers. And I am satisfied with either the steak dinner or a McDonald's hamburger.

137

That is sort of the way it is with sex. Sometimes it's like the steak, baked potato, rolls, and apple pie. At other times, it's just like McDonald's hamburgers. But it is always great. And it satisfies my needs and hers.

I hope you are reading this aloud and together as a couple — and that this will cause you to stop and talk about the whole area of the physical union, which is probably the most neglected area of communication between husbands and wives. It needs to be talked about at length, prayed over, and experienced together so that in a more full way each year, the two of you will truly become "one flesh."

Choosing the best (by Carole)

We drove along in silence for several miles. I could tell by the minuscule frown on her face that she was thinking deeply. The conversation had turned to marriage, and it was obvious that this wife of several years had a problem. As we left the city and the traffic thinned, she took a deep breath and said, "But how can I really keep my marriage exciting? Ours is a good marriage. We love each other. But somehow the fun, excitement, and sparkle have faded from our relationship. Is it possible to really keep the excitement in a marriage?"

As we talked, it became apparent that she had stopped doing a great many little things she had done at first. She didn't greet her husband at the door anymore with a smile and a kiss; she and her husband had stopped dating when the children came; someone else now took him to the airport for his trips and picked him up. But mainly it was their sex life that had become routine and dull. When the fun of sex evaporated into monotony, the little private jokes between them disappeared, and the electricity generated by both was cut off and no "sparks" remained. Exit excitement.

A unique, exciting physical relationship does not just happen. As in other areas of our marriages, it has to be worked at and planned for.

A woman has a difficult time separating love and sex. They are intertwined clear down to her inner being. At times a woman longs much more for the closeness and intimacy of the sex act than she does for the thrill of it. Most women long to be held, totally apart from sex. Understanding husbands need to be aware of the need for closeness that many wives have.

God created depths in the sexual area of our lives that few of us will ever plumb. It is difficult sometimes to keep God's perspective in a world that tries continually to make sex into one of the better body functions. One article to college students pointed out that it shouldn't hurt any more to break up after a fellow and girl had slept together than if they hadn't had intercourse. After all, the article said, it is just another body function. How sad! The shallowness of this point of view is leaving frustrated and despairing people in its wake.

God's plan is that sex will be like a deep, refreshing well with water that keeps springing up — invigorating, refreshing, pure. Solomon teaches us that when we make God's gift of sex impure, in other words, when we commit adultery and fornication, it is like stagnant, shallow water on the streets of our lives (see Proverbs 5:15-19).

Do we want the "muddy puddles" of casual sex or the "deep wells" that exist within the marriage relationship? We can't have it both ways. And the choice is ours. God will give us the deep wells to refresh our spirits and our bodies, wells that can be more beautiful with passing years. God wants a growing depth in our relationship together, and this is a "bottomless" well as far as I am concerned — one that can keep being explored with depths never reached. It has been said, "Sex is not something you do. Sex is something you are becoming together." And this is true.

Sex need never be boring or routine. God created us with a desire that is much like taking a long, cold drink of water on a hot summer afternoon. "Let your fountain be blessed, and rejoice in the wife of your youth. As a loving hind and a graceful doe, let her breasts satisfy you at all times; be exhilarated always with her love" (Proverbs 5:18-19, NASB).

Our God is a creative God. He can give us creative ideas in our sex lives. Do you ever pray for creativity from God in this area? You may. Do you ever pray that you will be a blessing to your mate in your physical relationship? You may. Do you ever ask God for His point of view when you experience hang-ups from your childhood? Do. God is interested in all our problems including those we have in this area.

One Old Testament phrase for intercourse is "to know." "Adam knew Eve his wife; and she conceived" (Genesis 4:1, KJV). This is a beautiful word because, to me, sex is total communication — body, soul, spirit. Total knowledge completes communication.

That's what it should be, but often it isn't.

140

Probably one of the first things a couple needs to do is to know and understand the facts. Many people have a terrible time just speaking out loud the correct name for parts of the body. Then they wonder why it is difficult for them to communicate about intimate areas of sex.

So, if you have never done it before, read a good marriage manual on sex aloud and together. Herbert Miles' *Sexual Happiness in Marriage,* Tim and Beverly LaHaye's *The Act of Marriage,* and Ed and Gaye Wheat's *Intended for Pleasure* are excellent and are written from a Christian point of view. Dr. Ed Wheat also has produced tapes that give a medical doctor's perspective.

Engaged couples should be encouraged to read these books separately during the engagement period and then aloud together a week or so before they are married. If they do this, it will enable them to begin to communicate in an area where so many can't get the words out of their mouths.

It is hard to believe that in this day of sex instruction in schools, on television, and in the movies, sex is still the number one matter couples have trouble talking about. Free and open discussion is essential. It is the first step on the road to "Excitement."

DISCUSSION QUESTIONS

- How did you learn about sex? What did you think?

- What has influenced your views about sex? The media? Friends? Experiences? Books?*

- How was sex treated in your family? Was it something secretive, or was your family comfortable talking about it?*

- After you're married, ask your spouse this question: "What would make me your ideal lover?"

- What's your sexual history? Have you shared it with your spouse?*

- What are/were your expectations for your wedding night?

- Read I Corinthians 6:16–7:16 in *The Message* and talk about it with your spouse. How can you let your spouse see God through your body?

- Read the Song of Songs. What stands out to you? Why? What do you see in the book that you'd like to apply to your own marriage?*

---

* *Questions ideal for journaling*

CHAPTER SIX

How You Celebrate

FOR BETTER OR WORSE

JOANNE:

In the first few years of our marriage, Christmas for us meant Interstate 25. Though our families lived only twenty minutes apart, it seemed that over the course of two days — Christmas Eve and Christmas Day — we spent hours in the car. From our house in Monument, Colorado, we would drive down I-25 for Christmas Eve dinner with Toben's family, up I-25 to spend the night with my family, down I-25 for Christmas dinner with Toben's family, up I-25 to see my family again.

Thanksgiving was worse. Not only did we put on the miles, we put on the pounds. Thanksgiving dinner with one family and dessert with the other somehow ends up being dinner and dessert with both. "Since it's not quite time for you to go to their house for dessert, how about just one piece of pie? I made your favorite — just for you." "Oh, you're here already? We're not finished with dinner yet. Are you sure you don't want to taste my turkey? I made it just the way you like it!"

We've figured out how to fix Thanksgiving — we just do our own thing. But we're still working on Christmas.

FOR BETTER OR WORSE

We were walking through our neighborhood the other night and talking about what we wanted to include in this chapter. While I love holidays, gifts, and surprises, we wanted this chapter to be about more than just that. We remembered our wedding vows and how we promised to stick with each other and love each other "for better or worse." *What does that really mean?* we wondered. The more we talked, the more we thought that, in part at least, it applies to celebrations.

How we celebrate the good times — birthdays, holidays, promotions, or new homes — affects how we handle the bad times too. As we go through our married life together, we set patterns in happy celebrations that give us a foundation for dealing with the hard times that come our way.

We saw this in action with Brian and Hanna, whom you've met in the pages of this book. With a particularly difficult week behind them, Hanna began Monday morning by rear-ending someone's car on the way to work. Not a great start to a week they hoped would be much better than the last. With her car in the shop and uncertain of the final repair bill, Brian and Hanna headed out for a nice dinner on Tuesday night to celebrate her new job. It seemed a little odd at first — after all, there was a car repair to pay for and another week with a bad start. But they were out celebrating. As Toben and I talked about it, we were struck by the importance of celebrating the best things that happen in marriage — even in the midst of the worst.

$\mathcal{T}$OBEN:

I couldn't agree more! I remember early in our marriage when Joanne and I got so bogged down in the difficulties we were facing that every fight seemed like the end of the world rather than a speed bump on an otherwise smooth road. During the first few years of our marriage, I had a tendency to be incredibly myopic. I focused on whatever big bad thing was lurking out there instead of seeing things in view of the rest of our lives together.

Every financial setback or relational pothole loomed large for me. I was so "in the moment" that I didn't think about the fifty or sixty years I hope we will have together to figure it out. This was especially true of money.

As we mentioned earlier, we got deep into debt quickly after getting married. As a result, every raise or bonus represented more money that we could send to the credit card. I remember thinking at one point, "We are making pretty decent money, but we are living like we're nearly broke." We wanted to be out of debt so badly that everything went to pay it off, and we continued to live hand-to-mouth.

Eventually we realized that if we didn't take advantage of the opportunities to celebrate little victories that came along, we were never going to survive. We needed the relief that little celebrations bring to otherwise difficult days. So we started taking a portion of the bonuses I earned from time to time and spending them to have fun. We would eat out or head to the mountains for a couple of days. Doing those little things made everything feel better. The problems we faced certainly didn't evaporate, but having a little fun helped us keep them in perspective.

FIRST STEPS

What's something your family always celebrated?

Brian: As far as big events in our family, it's always been Christmas. Our extended family always comes to our house. One year we had eighteen people in our house for Christmas. Of course, it was the year that fourteen of those people got stomach flu on Christmas Eve. Luckily, I was one of the ones who didn't get it.

Hanna: Graduations have always been a big deal in my family. We have a bonfire at each graduation that we build on top of the remains of the previous one. They're huge!

HOLIDAYS

JOANNE:

We were talking with some friends recently who were about to get married. We asked what potential problems they thought they might face. "How are you going to celebrate Christmas?" we asked. "Whose family will you spend it with?" They looked at us blankly. "We haven't even thought about it," they said.

Traditions and holidays might not seem like a big deal when compared with communication, finances, and sex. But how you celebrate events in life can be a place where expectations go unmet. And for many people, holidays can be stressful enough without adding another person's traditions to the mix.

Chances are, your families celebrate differently. Even though Toben's family and mine are similar on the outside, how we handled birthdays, gifts, Christmas, and other holidays growing up is very different.

I could easily relate to Larry Miller when he wrote about the differences in gift-giving at Christmas time: "When we were dating, Kathy commented during our first Christmas together, 'You only have one present?' I didn't think it was odd until I saw the multitude of presents under Kathy's tree. It seemed to me they really overdid it."[1]

Like Kathy's family, my family goes a little overboard at Christmas, with gifts spilling out from under the tree, around the room, and wherever there's clear space on the floor. Opening presents (one by one from the youngest to the oldest) usually takes several hours. Toben's family buys only a few gifts per person.

The kinds of gifts our families buy are different too. I love surprises. I don't want to know what you bought me for Christmas. Don't even give me a hint. For me, even the possibility of figuring out what's in the box takes all the fun out of it. I want to be completely and totally surprised. And if I'm giving a gift, I want the person to whom I'm giving it to be surprised too.

Toben, on the other hand, isn't into surprises. In my family, everyone surprises everyone else. But Toben's family has always used Christmas lists. You ask for what you want, and that's what you get — well, most of the time anyway. Needless to say, that took some getting used to for me — especially when Toben wants something I just don't understand.

GIVING GIFTS

Toben is easy to shop for — if you're loaded with money and don't mind buying him something he already has. He loves expensive things —

fountain pens, watches, pocketknives, and leather goods — and has a lot of them. So when he told me he wanted a pocketknife for Father's Day, I was resigned to get it for him. Until I saw it.

To me, a pocketknife is of the Swiss Army variety — but the knife he wanted only had one blade. Nary a toothpick, tweezer, or corkscrew in sight. To me, it looked like you could kill someone with it. And it looked a lot like the one he'd bought just a few weeks before.

I bought him a cordless drill instead. It's pretty neat and he does like it, but I feel kind of bad that I didn't get him what he really wanted.

Remember the episode of *The Simpsons* where Homer buys Marge a bowling ball for her birthday? If I remember correctly, it even had his name on it. How often have I bought gifts for Toben out of a selfish motivation ("Gee, I'd really like to have this, so I'll buy it for him and borrow it.") instead of thinking of him first?

*T*OBEN:

Joanne is easy to shop for — if spending a lot of time in the housewares department is your idea of fun. Joanne often wants things that to me seem unromantic and unlike what a husband should buy a wife at birthdays or Christmas. I like to buy her jewelry. But I know that the gifts she has loved the most are terribly practical. I bought her new dishes for Christmas two years ago and she went nuts for that. For her birthday a few months ago, we got her a KitchenAid mixer, which is really just a glorified blender. She went crazy!

Also, I have always related the cost of the gift with the sentiment behind it. If I spend a ton of money, then Joanne will know that I really love her. But Joanne loves little inexpensive gifts — stationery, candles, and anything from The Container Store. It's taken me years to accept that I can honor Joanne with little gifts and that I don't have to spend hundreds of dollars to make her happy.

*J*OANNE:

So, what's the point of all this? I think the point we're trying to make is that while giving and receiving gifts may not seem like a big deal, it's another part of your marriage where you have the opportunity to know your spouse and demonstrate that knowledge.

Incidentally, you might consider keeping a list handy to make a note of things your partner would like to receive as gifts. This is invaluable — especially if your spouse is hard to shop for.

149

First Steps

Would you rather be surprised or get something you asked for?

Hanna: I'd rather get something I asked for. One time we were shopping and I'd seen a jacket that I wanted so badly. And one day Brian just drove home with it hanging from the dry cleaning hook. But when he does buy me something I want, he usually can't wait until my birthday or Christmas to give it to me. So that day I don't have anything to open!

Brian: I don't even know. Is it possible to be surprised with what you really want? On Wednesday, Hanna gave me two CDs I'd mentioned that I wanted four or five weeks earlier. Maybe that's the ultimate — being surprised with what I asked for.

MERGING TRADITIONS

If you go at it with creativity and a good attitude, merging your traditions can be one of the most fun things about being married. No, you probably can't celebrate each holiday, birthday, and job promotion with each of your families the way they celebrate those things. But you can merge your traditions to come up with something even more memorable.

The other day Toben's mother, Pamela, was telling me how she celebrated one Thanksgiving. Her in-laws lived in Pennsylvania and didn't travel to Colorado very often. It was a rare occasion when they were able to spend holidays together. So in the week that they visited for Thanksgiving, they celebrated all the holidays at once.

One night was Easter. Pamela made a big ham, got out the kids' Easter baskets, and decorated for Easter. Another night was everyone's birthday. She threw a birthday party, decorated with party favors, and made a birthday cake big enough for everyone. On Thanksgiving (which it actually was), she decorated for Thanksgiving, made turkey with all the trimmings, and finished the meal with pumpkin pie. And before they left, they decorated the Christmas tree and celebrated Christmas together.

"It was a lot of work," Pamela told me, "but what fun! Lowell's dad still talks about it — years later."

It can take a while to merge your family traditions. But it's possible. After being married for many years, Jack and Carole Mayhall say, "We've joined our traditions to make a year rich with celebrations." But that joining of traditions didn't happen right away:

We ran into the . . . problem our very first Christmas. Carole wanted to wait until Christmas morning to open gifts! Can you believe that? Every sane person knows that Christmas Eve is the time to gather around the tree and open gifts. But no. Christmas Eve, said Carole, was the time to have the Christmas story and sing carols. And then early Christmas morning, one woke in excited anticipation of stockings filled with goodies. After a hurried breakfast, the gifts would be opened one by one with each taking a turn giving out a gift to another. It took her family hours, and Christmas dinner was forgotten in the process. Imagine that! No traditional Christmas dinner.

And Christmas wasn't the only holiday we celebrated in divergent ways. There was Valentine's Day (she celebrated it, I didn't); Easter (a new outfit was essential but she had to wear it Palm Sunday so she wouldn't think about the new clothes on Easter; I can never remember having a new outfit); and the Fourth of July (big family reunion for Carole; fireworks in the park for me).[2]

So what about you? What holidays do you celebrate? What about your spouse? (Don't wait till the last minute to make your holiday plans—especially if your families live near each other!) How can you join your traditions together and create your own unique way of celebrating?

Having Fun

How do you celebrate the smaller things in life? A new job? A day where everything goes right? A new friend? How can we keep from falling into a routine where we fail to celebrate—fail to have fun?

In Jan Karon's best-selling Mitford Series, Father Tim struggles with these same questions. After getting married at the age of sixty, he and his wife, Cynthia, are quickly caught up in the everyday busyness of their lives.

> *What they needed, he thought, was an adventure, some recreation. Hadn't they agreed on that very thing not long after their honeymoon? He had boldly declared they'd do something interesting every weekend, even in the dead of winter. In fact, they'd shaken hands on it.*
>
> *But what were they doing? Why, working, of course. And falling into bed like two logs, with scarcely a fare-thee-well. . . .*
>
> *There was nothing for it but to come up with a whole new ball game in the area of recreation.[3]*

Toben and I seem to go through two distinct phases: one where we do the same old same old, day in and day out, and one where we're constantly having fun. The challenge, like Father Tim found, was to bring the fun into every day.

I think it's best to start small. When we were dating, Toben and I often went to the park to swing. I love to swing. And best of all, it's free and it's fun. Swinging for just five or ten minutes can give me a whole new perspective and can completely brighten my day. Visiting the zoo, walking around an expensive neighborhood to look at houses and landscaping, or taking the dogs for a swim in the pond — all of these things are fun and add something to our marriage.

The first summer after we were married, we were living on campus in a tiny apartment with no air-conditioning and only two windows. It was a particularly hot summer, and it cooled off only into the high seventies at night. We were sweltering. During the day, we'd look at every kind of ice cream Safeway had to offer as we hung as far into the freezer case as possible. At night, we'd get out of the shower without drying off and stand in front of the fan trying to get cool. On top of that, we seemed to be dealing with one big issue after another. The heat was stifling — and we felt stifled by each other. Not a great combination.

As hard as that summer was in many ways, that was the summer we learned how to have fun in the midst of difficulty. We'd declare tomorrow a fun day, vow to put our disagreement aside for the day, and head to the lake. We'd leave early in the morning, pack a picnic, find a secluded little beach, and swim all day. At the end of the day, we'd stop for Slurpees and sing with the radio the rest of the way home. 153

Our fun days didn't make our disagreements (or the heat) go away. But they did teach us how to put things aside for an hour, a day, or a weekend in order to remember why we fell in love in the first place.

Are some issues in your relationship stifling you from celebrating life and each other? Do you feel like you've become stuck in a "worse" rut and can't quite remember the "better" in your marriage? It's time to have some fun and celebrate the good things in your relationship.

First Steps

What do you do for fun?

Brian: We go to the dollar movies.

Hanna: And then the hot tub at our apartment. Or sometimes we'll cook a special dinner just to celebrate nothing in particular.

"HAPPY I LOVE YOU DAYS" AND
OTHER CELEBRATIONS

It started with Slurpees. I love Slurpees — especially the peach flavor. And peach is hard to find. So one day when Toben found a 7-Eleven with peach Slurpees, he brought one to me at work to brighten my day — and "Happy I Love You Days" were born. Sometimes they come with a certain frequency, and other times they're few and far between. Being on the receiving end of a "Happy I Love You Day" is great fun, and being on the giving end is even more fun. A funny card or a serious note, a small gift or an extravagant one — doing something to show your spouse you care is exciting. Having "Happy I Love You Days" has helped Toben and me pay more attention to the little things that bring each other joy.

Just a few weeks ago I was showered with "Happy I Love You Days." From Dove bars to an antique treadle sewing machine, Toben told me and showed me how much he loves me. It left me feeling special and wanting to show him how much I love him too.

So what kinds of traditions have other couples started? From stockings at Christmas to carving pumpkins each fall, the kinds of traditions we found are numerous. Some friends always make a point to see the flybys at the Air Force Academy. Others never miss fireworks on New Year's Eve.

One couple we talked to has a cookie party every Christmas. They bake cookies and then invite all their friends over to help decorate them. They provide gift boxes so their friends can take their cookies home and give them as gifts.

154

Celebrating Others

One of the traditions that Toben and I have been purposeful about is the tradition of celebrating others. We want people to feel welcome and at home in our house. Whether we invited you for dinner a week in advance or five minutes before you walked in the door, we want you to feel free to relax and rest in our home.

A while back, we built a new house — one with quite a bit more space than we had previously. We finished the basement recently, giving us a private suite — bedroom, bathroom, and sitting room. As we were completing the work in the basement, we talked often about how excited we were to see who God would bring to stay there. We feel strongly that our house is really God's house, and we want Him to use it however He chooses.

There's a verse in Hebrews that makes me more and more enthusiastic to live in an "open" house: "Be ready with a meal or a bed when it's needed. Why, some have extended hospitality to angels without ever knowing it!" (Hebrews 13:2). How thrilling! Won't it be fun to get to heaven someday and see who we've entertained?

I can't help thinking of Abraham and Sarah in the book of Genesis. What would have happened if they'd turned away the strangers who showed up for a meal — the strangers who told them that Isaac would be born? How would they have found out the happy news if they hadn't been so open with their hospitality?

The writer of Hebrews goes on to say this: "Share what you have with others. God takes particular pleasure in acts of worship — a different kind of 'sacrifice' — that take place in kitchen and workplace and on the streets" (Hebrews 13:16).

In the past I've often thought that I didn't have anything to offer God — I can't sing a solo during the offering; I'm not rich enough to build Him a church building; I've not been called to go to Africa as a missionary. But I can offer God this "different kind of sacrifice" — sharing what I have, opening my home to others — in which He takes "particular pleasure."

*T*OBEN:

Joanne definitely has the gift of hospitality. I have the gift of service. I love to help out in any way I can, whenever I can. Most frequently that means helping people move. It seems like not a month goes by that some of our friends are buying a house or moving into a new apartment. And as strange as it sounds, I almost always love to help. Joanne's folks have the biggest pickup truck I've ever seen, and they are great about letting me use it to haul other people's stuff. It sure beats renting a moving van or making multiple trips back and forth across town.

For a while there was a crew of about eight of us who would show up to help couples from our Sunday school class move. We would time how long it would take us to get the truck loaded, drive to the new house, and unload. Our record was just under two hours. We always had a blast.

And new couples to our class were always surprised when we all showed up to lug their stuff. Service is a great way to celebrate others and to remember what God calls us to do in their lives. It seems like Joanne and I always get along best when we are inviting people into our home or getting out of the house to help others.

In *All* Things Give Thanks

*J*OANNE:

In 1997, Toben spent the entire month of May in the hospital. After one surgery and a week in the hospital, we thought everything was fixed, so he came home. In a day and a half, he was back in the emergency room and rushed into surgery. The doctor advised against further tests, believing that there wasn't time to wait for the results. If we waited, he informed us, Toben could die.

I spent the month in a chair next to Toben's bed. The company I worked for was extremely flexible and allowed me to work from the hospital. At the time, I was editing a compilation of three of Carole Mayhall's books.[4] It seemed that no matter what part of the book I was working on, it was about giving thanks to God — and not just for the good stuff. It was about thanking God for everything — even the things we don't want and can't stand.

I tried to reason away what God was obviously telling me loud and clear. *It's not like I'm reading this for me,* I thought. *This is work.* I'd read about how Carole learned to thank God when she spilled paint all over the floor. *Paint is one thing,* I'd reason. *This is my husband's life.*

But then the idea of giving thanks started popping up all over the place. Conversations with friends about how I was holding up would invariably turn to thanking God for the hard times. Something I'd hear on the radio would trigger the thought of giving thanks for difficulties.

I gave up. *Okay, God. I'm listening.* And He assured me that He wasn't kidding — He really wanted me to thank Him for everything we were going through. Little by little, I did. Oh, it didn't come right away. And I don't think I really meant it the first time I prayed it. But over the course of that May and the months that followed, God taught me a lesson. When I thank Him for the difficult things that come my way, He gives me joy — and a peace that really does pass all understanding.

IN SUMMARY

The early days of our marriage were filled with some real highs and lows. If we hadn't made the most of the highs, the lows would have seemed much more difficult. A number of authors have written about "emotional bank accounts" where we make deposits and withdrawals all the time. I think the same is true for good times and bad times.

158   When we celebrate the good times, it's like saving for a rainy day. It gives us a little something in reserve that allows us to get through some of the dark days that come in every marriage. And from time to time, we have to manufacture a celebration in order to break up the pattern of tough stuff that gets thrown at us.

Spend some time talking about birthdays, holidays, and everyday celebrations. Decide how you want to celebrate things in your marriage. And above all, don't forget to have some fun!

∞

VOICE OF WISDOM

I (Joanne) had lunch with my friend Jan Maniatis today to talk about celebration. She's one of those people who is always thinking of other people and doing little things to make others feel special and loved.

This is the second marriage for both Jan and her husband, Bob, so merging traditions for them meant merging their own family backgrounds and merging the traditions their grown children grew up with.

"Bob grew up without the significance of Christ in traditions," Jan says. "That was the biggest difference in our family backgrounds. That made our celebrations very different."

Something else that has made their celebrations different from those of many young couples is the fact that when they remarried, none of their parents were living. "It was hard when we got married," Jan says. "Both Bob and I are only children, so we didn't have family to celebrate with us. We wanted to make some sort of connection with our parents and have them be part of our celebration even though they were gone. We bought a bouquet of balloons, attached a note to each one, and let them go. We were surprised at how poignant it was, and we both cried and cried. But it made the cele-bration of our marriage more meaningful.

"Because our parents weren't living, we didn't have to decide at whose house to spend the holidays. But we did have to merge our children and their holiday celebrations."

Merging Christmas traditions has been the most complicated holiday merging Jan and Bob have faced. "Bob's family opened gifts on Christmas Eve, but for me that ruins Christmas morning. Still, he's pliable about those kinds of things and lets me push things to where I like them."

And merging those Christmas traditions and preferences can get overwhelming. "For a while, Christmas got out of hand," Jan admits. "I let everyone pick a favorite dish, and I made it part of our Christmas dinner. One year we had turkey *and* ham."

With two sets of children, it's important to Jan for them to feel appreciated and wanted. "Our kids have never all been together on Christmas — they usually take turns. The challenge is trying to figure out how to make the time they spend with us special. I try to think of something that will let them know they're important to me — a favorite food or tradition. And with Bob's children it's a challenge to do that without infringing on what their mom would do."

The other holiday challenge Jan continually faces is Bob's work schedule. "Because of Bob's work at the post office, he comes home on Christmas Eve just exhausted, knowing he has to go back the day after Christmas," she says. "I want to do things to make him feel like he had a Christmas.

"I have a tendency to capitalize on the tiny moments, which is a whole new concept to him. I think it's important to celebrate those little moments, things like a really good day or a really bad day. And I love doing those little things, those unexpected things that make someone's day."

While Jan was raising her two children as a single mom, she tried to celebrate those little things too. "When we received our income tax return, everyone got something they really wanted. Nothing practical, but something fun."

As we talk about celebrations, I'm struck by how much Jan strives to celebrate who Bob is as a person. "In business, we try to catch people doing right. In marriage, I think it's important to do the same thing," she says. "There are things about Bob that really attracted me to him at first, and I try to celebrate those things in him when I see them in action.

"It's easy to begin to pick at your spouse—those things that drive you crazy! This can really begin to chip away at the foundation you are trying to build. Instead of concentrating on these social faux pas or irritating little habits, pick a good thing and praise your spouse for that. You'll be surprised at how much it does for your attitude and the gratefulness you feel for your spouse."

One of those things that Jan tries to celebrate is Bob's focus and ability to work hard. "Bob doesn't get positive feedback in his work environment, and that's hard. So I do things to let him know that I value him and his hard work," she says. "After all, those things make him the person he is."

So what kinds of things does she do? Here's her "quick-to-do" list:

- Buy balloons. They're cheap, festive, and fun. And they're great for work or any environment.
- Set the table. Candles, cloth napkins, and china make the meat-loaf seem better.

- Write anytime love notes. Drive by your spouse's office and leave a note on the windshield to be found at lunch.
- Serve hors d'oeuvres on the deck. Eating outside somehow adds perspective to the day.
- Have a pizza party in bed.
- Send a card. You can find the perfect one for any and every occasion.
- Give candy. Leave a candy bar for your spouse with an appropriate note. For M&Ms, "You're MMMM." For Milky Way, "You're the star of my universe." And so on.
- Leave "I miss you" love notes. If you go on a business trip, leave notes for your partner to find. Try leaving Post-it Notes on the pillow or the coffee pot, or write in lipstick on the mirror.

Discussion Questions

- Describe a memorable birthday from when you were young. What makes it stand out in your mind? Was this a typical way for your family to celebrate birthdays? Why, or why not?

- What's your favorite holiday? Why? How can you and your spouse continue to make this holiday unique?*

- Do you like to receive gifts you've asked for, or would you rather be surprised?

- For which holidays do you plan to buy gifts for each other? Christmas? Valentine's Day? Birthday? What about for other family members?

- What are some things that you could thank God for — both the good and the difficult?*

- What is one of your family's nonholiday traditions that you want to continue in your marriage? Why?

- What kinds of gifts does your partner like to receive? Practical or impractical? Surprises or what he or she asked for?

- What are some ways that you can bring an element of fun into your everyday lives?

- How do you react to a crisis?

- What's a holiday you could invent and celebrate together?*

- Should you set a spending limit for gifts? What should that limit be?

- Describe a difficult time you've been through as a couple. What did God teach you through that situation?*

---

* Questions *ideal for journaling*

CHAPTER SEVEN

How You Connect

THE VALUE OF COMMUNITY

JOANNE:

We've told part of this story already, but here's the whole thing. I was on my way out the door to the airport when the phone rang. Toben was due home from a business trip in Los Angeles, and I was anxious for him to arrive. "The flight's been cancelled from Denver," he said. "And I don't feel very well."

By the time the passengers were bussed to Colorado Springs from Denver, it was after midnight. I sat in the car in my pajamas, impatient and tired. Toben got in the car and immediately doubled over, screaming in pain. My exhaustion was replaced by panic as we raced to the emergency room.

After surgery, ten days in the hospital, a day and a half at home, a second emergency surgery to repair damage done from the first, and another three weeks in the hospital, we came home to an empty fridge and more than $100,000 in medical bills. We had insurance, but it didn't cover everything, which left us worried about how to come up with several thousand dollars — fast.

For the past nine months or so, we'd been involved in a small group with four other couples. We'd committed to building a community among ourselves based on what we saw in the book of Acts:

And all the believers lived in a wonderful harmony, holding everything in common. They sold whatever they owned and pooled their resources so that each person's need was met.

They followed a daily discipline of worship in the Temple followed by meals at home, every meal a celebration, exuberant and joyful, as they praised God (2:44-47).

166

We met together weekly for Bible study, ate dinner before the study as one big family, and helped each other move and paint. We prayed for one another each day and loved each other deeply.

When the members of this small group came to visit after Toben finally came home from the hospital, they brought a card — and a check for almost $1,000.

WHAT IS COMMUNITY?

Community is more than just a group of people spending time together. I'm sure I'm not the only one who's ever been in a room full of people yet felt left out and lonely. So what turns a group of people into a community?

I think three main ingredients make up a community. In Philippians, Paul tells his readers in a nutshell the secret to community: "If you've gotten any-

thing at all out of following Christ, if his love has made any difference in your life, if being in a community of the Spirit means anything to you, if you have a heart, if you care — then do me a favor: Agree with each other, love each other, be deep-spirited friends" (2:1-2).

"Agree with each other, love each other, be deep-spirited friends." It couldn't be easier, right? Wrong. I think it's important to look at what Paul really meant by each of these things in order to understand how together they make a community.

Agree with each other. Unfortunately, when most of us see this verse we tend to think that it means people should agree with us. We don't often think that it means we should agree with someone else — especially when that person's opinion is the exact opposite of ours.

I think Paul is talking about more than agreeing with opinions here. In order to create community, agreeing with each other means agreeing to put forth effort to build a community. What is the purpose of your group? To learn? To hold each other accountable? To have fun? Expectations don't apply only to marriage — each member of a community has expectations of what that community will be like. Agreeing on the purpose of your community is the first step to building an authentic one.

Love each other. Community, like marriage, involves commitment. Part of agreeing with each other about the purpose of your community is to agree with each other about how long your community will last. Whatever you decide, that agreement includes a commitment to stick with it until it's over. Without that commitment, it's hard to help your community grow.

Loving each other isn't always easy. But knowing that the other members aren't going to walk away when the going gets tough makes it easier to do the hard work of loving each other. James knew that loving each other is vital for community: "You can develop a healthy, robust community that lives right with God and enjoy its results *only* if you do the hard work of getting along with each other, treating each other with dignity and honor" (James 3:18). According to James, you can't have a healthy community without loving each other — even when you don't feel like it.

Be deep-spirited friends. This is the part of community that everyone wants to get to. It's why a healthy community is so appealing when we see it in action. Paul mentions it last because deep-spirited friendships don't come without the work of agreeing with and loving each other. It's the promise of these kinds of friendships that keeps us going through the work of community.

168

But the work doesn't stop there. In Galatians, Paul describes what comes next: "Right now, therefore, every time we get the chance, let us work for the benefit of all, starting with the people closest to us in the community of faith" (6:10).

And that's the ultimate purpose of community when it comes right down to it — working for the benefit of all.

We've been fortunate enough to experience this kind of community a few times, but it wasn't easy to find and didn't happen right away.

HELP! WE NEED FRIENDS

*T*OBEN:

After Joanne and I had been married a couple of years, we really started to feel alone. Even though we had each other, something was missing.

We had friends, but most of them were from our places of work. We would all go out and talk about — you guessed it — work. And most of them were older or single. None of them were at the stage we were in life. No one really got what we were about or what we were going through as a young married couple — learning to juggle our time together and our time at work, deciding whether and when to have a family, and so on. We were desperate for community.

At the time, we were attending a church that wasn't very community-oriented. People would show up on Sundays, participate in worship, and go home. Don't get me wrong, the worship was reverential and powerful in a way that Joanne and I hadn't experienced before, and for a time it really met a deeply felt need. But we were starving for community.

One Sunday we skipped church and went grocery shopping. Our intention, at least, was to skip church. On the way back from the store we drove past a church that's less than a mile from our house — a church we'd driven past at least twice each day. We looked at each other and both felt compelled to worship there that Sunday. What we discovered there was a church that had Christ at its center and a strong commitment to community.

We started attending regularly. At that time there were no Sunday school classes or small groups for young couples, so we talked to one of the pastors at the church about starting a class. He was supportive and connected us with a few other young married couples in the church who were also looking to make friends and have a ministry.

After getting to know a few of those couples, we met for the first time as the "Young Couples Without Kids" Sunday school class. Long name, but it was pretty clear to anyone who saw the class listing in the bulletin what we were all about.

As the weeks progressed, more and more couples showed up until there were about thirty of us on any given Sunday. We started a few Bible studies out of that group, and deep and lasting relationships began to form.

Almost every couple who came to the class articulated a common need — they were desperate for relationships and community. The few of us who started the class were determined to make every couple who walked through our door on Sundays feel welcome. We would often invite all the first-timers to lunch after class, and if they weren't available, we would do our best to share a meal with them sometime during that same week.

Our friends Doug and Lisa are the best I've ever seen at making people feel valued and welcomed. They connected with new couples in such a genuine way that almost every couple who came once came back again and again. Because of Doug and Lisa and our commitment as a group to make people feel included, we found our community.

A TIME TO COCOON

We know that not every newly married couple feels the need to connect with other couples as soon as their vows are said. In fact, we didn't feel that need for community until we'd been married for several years.

Joanne and I have some friends who did almost nothing their first year of marriage except spend time together. Kevin and Mary tried to take Deuteronomy 24:5 literally: "If a man has recently married, he must not be sent to war or have any other duty laid on him. For one year he is to be free to stay at home and bring happiness to the wife he has married" (NIV).

Kevin and Mary had been incredibly busy in their last year of college at Louisiana State University and wanted to do nothing more than spend time with one another. Kevin was headed to seminary, and they knew that would be a crazy time. So they made sure that between one busy season and the next, they would lay the groundwork for a close, connected marriage.

There is definitely a season for cocooning. According to trend analyst Faith Popcorn, "Cocooning is about insulation and avoidance, peace and protection, coziness and control — a sort of hyper-nesting."[1] With that definition, it makes sense that newly married couples do it. After all, the first year of marriage is a time to nest — settle in to your new life together, build a home, and be together.

During college, a number of other couples were married and the joke was always, "Now that they're married, we'll never see them again." And for many of those couples, that was true. They were certainly having more fun at home than they could have at the student union! But another season follows, probably at a different time for every couple, when they're ready to get out and meet new people or reconnect with old friends.

And a Time to Connect

I think that when Joanne and I were first married, we thought to some extent that the other person was the human embodiment of everything we needed, relationally speaking. In those early days, you could have dropped us on a deserted island somewhere and we wouldn't have panicked because we thought we needed only each other — and we'd continue to need only each other.

But you can't be all things to your spouse, no matter how you may try. If you do try, you will likely make your partner crazy and yourself miserable. Your spouse is the one person in the world who is capable of fulfilling the greatest percentage of your needs. But all those met needs simply can't add up to 100 percent. Joanne and I both came to a realization a couple of months into our married life that we couldn't be all things to each other.

172   Joanne plays golf, very occasionally. But I like to play pretty often. If Joanne is the only person I can go with, someone is going to be pretty ticked off most of the time. Joanne is an arts and crafts devotee, but if I have to go to Hobby Lobby more than once a year, I break out in hives.

This principle applies to more than just activities and interests. We need other people around us to stimulate our thinking, to challenge us in ways that our spouse may not. There are great examples of friendships in Scripture — Jonathan and David, Ruth and Naomi. Jonathan filled needs in David's life that multiple wives simply couldn't!

I mentioned before that my friend Steve and I used to get together once a week to pray and hold each other accountable for various things. After a couple of weeks of doing so, Joanne said, "I don't know what you and Steve are talking about, but I can really see a difference in you." I was changing in some ways Joanne had hoped I would. But she hadn't known how to bring those issues up, or perhaps she was just too close to them. Steve was an interested third party who did a lot to improve our marriage.

I know Joanne has received help and encouragement from her friends as well. The point is that we need all kinds of people in our lives.

First Steps

What are some needs you have that are better met by friends?

Hanna: Sometimes I really need to be a freak and hype out, and sometimes Brian doesn't appreciate that. Luckily I have friends who appreciate that and can be completely crazy with me. Since we've been here, I'm still finding friends who meet that need.

Brian: I don't know that there are needs Hanna can't meet so much as there are things that can only be fulfilled by me being alone. There are little things like talking about music, movies, and concerts. But for the most part it's the need to be alone.

Knitting Needles and Glue Guns

*J*OANNE:

Toben mentioned my love for Hobby Lobby, but in truth, I haven't been there in months. (Having kids has definitely changed that aspect of my life!) But he's right about one thing — if I wanted to go with someone, he sure wouldn't be the one to go with me.

It's not really his fault that he doesn't get excited about making wreaths, putting together scrapbooks, or finding knitting needles for a

173

new knitting project. After all, men and women are different. And while there are a lot of things we enjoy doing together (even golf every once in a while!), there are some things we just don't have in common.

When we were first engaged, we didn't think it was okay that we had separate interests. During our first year at Whitworth College, we did everything together. If I wanted to be on the yearbook staff, Toben would join too. And if he wanted to take a certain class, it was a given that I'd enroll for it too. In a way, we did a lot of our cocooning during our engagement.

But after we were married, we both felt a wonderful sense of freedom to explore our own interests — on our own. Toben ran for student government (something I had no interest in at all), and I began editing the college newspaper (something he rarely even read). We learned that we couldn't always have the same interests and that it was okay for us to explore life without the other. The important thing was that we ended up in the same place when the day was done. And it was so much fun to lie in bed at night and talk about what each of us had done that day.

During that time, we made a lot of new friends that we wouldn't have made otherwise. In pursuing our own interests, we found other people who could enjoy those things with us.

YOURS, MINE, AND OURS

*T*OBEN:

Joanne and I have a lot of friends. She has her friends, I have mine, and we have ours. The relationships we build with our individual friends are no different from the friendships we have built throughout our lives.

But the friendships we are building together are more challenging — and more rewarding — than any other friendships we have.

Yes, those relationships are hard to find and complicated to develop. You can do the math. If there is one relationship between each person, then there is one friendship between Joanne and a close friend. In a friendship of couples, the sum is six. The number of relationships represented by each of the marriages is two. There are four relationships between the couples. So "couple" relationships are three times as complicated as friendships between two people. (Our editor suggested we have an accountant work on our figures, but I think you get the point!)

I can think of a couple of friendships in particular that have been a real blessing. Ann is one of Joanne's best friends from high school. They have an amazing relationship. They see each other rarely and only have time to call each other once a month or so. But every time they get together or talk on the phone it's like they've never been apart. Ann met and married a great guy named Bill. They met in law school in Boston, and Joanne and I were fortunate enough to get to spend time with them while they were still dating. Whenever we see them we have a blast, and we value our friendship with them very much.

Our friends Brian and Hanna went to college at Whitworth, just as Joanne and I did. Brian and I have known each other for years because he and my cousin Kate have been friends for as long as I can remember. Last Christmas, Brian was home on break and mentioned that he was desperate to find a job in Colorado Springs. He and Hanna planned to be married in a few months, and he wanted to find a job and an apartment for them before the big day rolled around. Fortunately for both of us, there was an opening at my company and Brian started almost right away.

When he and Hanna got married, I was there. After their honeymoon, they moved here, and we've been close ever since. In many ways, we're writing this book for them and for other people who are at the same place in life as they are. They've been a great source of encouragement as we've talked about this book. And more than that, they've reminded us what life in the first year of marriage is all about. They are madly in love.

There are a few other couples who have invested a lot in us, and vice versa. They're the people who we live our lives with. At times we may see each other a few times a week, while at other times we're lucky to be together once a month. But either way, those friendships are some of the relationships I value most.

YOUR MARRIAGE A LIGHTHOUSE

NavPress published a book a number of years ago called *Your Home a Lighthouse* by Bob and Betty Jacks. Their thesis is that through inviting nonChristians into our homes for Bible study, we can make an impact on them for Christ. I couldn't agree more. We can have an impact even without a formal Bible study. Everywhere we go and in everything we do, we have that same opportunity in our marriages — and not only in our marriages, but in the Christian communities that we form.

When I was in the hospital, one of the nurses who regularly attended to me said, "I don't know what it is, but there is something different about your room. It's not like any of the other rooms on the ward. It feels like there is a lot of love in here." That may have had something to do with the fact that we were surrounded, embraced, and supported by our community. It was actually tangible to those outside looking in.

Community is inviting. It's something other people want to be a part of when they see it in action. Don't be afraid to invite people who don't yet know Jesus to participate with you in community — whether in the small community of two in your marriage or in the larger community you find in other friends. That is relational evangelism at its finest — when not just one but a number of people can share their lives with an unbeliever who can look in on the difference faith makes.

Your marriage is an example to those around you and a great opportunity for lifestyle evangelism. We're called to be salt and light:

177

> "Let me tell you why you are here. You're here to be salt-seasoning that brings out the God-flavors of this earth. If you lose your saltiness, how will people taste godliness? You've lost your usefulness and will end up in the garbage.
>
> "Here's another way to put it: You're here to be light, bringing out the God-colors in the world. God is not a secret to be kept. We're going public with this, as public as a city on a hill. If I make you light-bearers, you don't think I'm going to hide you under a bucket, do you? I'm putting you on a light stand. Now that I've put you there on a hilltop, on a light stand — shine! Keep open house; be generous with your lives. By opening up to others, you'll prompt people to open up with God, this generous Father in heaven" (Matthew 5:13-16).

Just as one granule of salt or one candle represents salt and light, imagine how much better a whole teaspoon of salt or a whole grouping of candles is at fulfilling this purpose. That's what community can do.

You Get What You Give

Imagine that at every gift-giving holiday, you got the gift that you gave. If you bought your wife pajamas, you would receive those exact pajamas when you opened your present. If you bought her a blender, in the package intended for you would be a blender. After a while you'd figure it out and buy your wife a table saw or a new set of golf clubs!

That's how community works. You get back what you give. Joanne and I have seen couples spend years waiting for community to happen to them. They bounce from church to church, attending different small groups and Bible studies, waiting for community magically to appear. It'll never happen.

Community, by its nature and definition, is active. To participate in community you have to be active too. Even if you're lucky enough to find an active community in a church you attend, you can't expect to just show up and become a part of what's going on. You have to listen, you have to disclose, you have to invest, and you have to be willing to be invested in. Take the initiative. Community won't fall in your lap. Invite a couple from work, church, or the neighborhood over for dinner; join (or start) a small group or Sunday school class.

Joanne and I have seen community that worked and attempts at community that missed the mark. The community that we mentioned at the beginning of this chapter was full of people who were committed to engaging others and investing in one another. There was an incredible desire to connect. The friendships that began in that group almost three years ago are still vital today.

One of the things that we did every time we got together was eat a meal. We took the Acts 2 model of the church seriously and in that passage there was food, so we had food. Each couple involved brought one thing essential to the meal. No one ever forgot or just decided not to bring anything. There was always enough food, and we had a great time around the table together.

Recently a bunch of us at the new church we attend decided to take the summer to get together and build community among the twenty-somethings in our congregation. We decided to do the food thing as part of our time together. To get things started, Kim, Kevin, and I provided most of the food the first week. We had a barbecue and a hundred people showed up! We asked for people to help provide food the next week. A couple of people did. The third week there was almost no food at all. And we couldn't find volunteers to help with setup, teardown, music, promotion, or anything else.

Our last meeting was last week, and no one showed up except the leadership team. And we provided all the food again. While the larger group didn't gel, the ten of us have become a community. Somehow that didn't transfer to the rest of the people who had joined us the first few weeks. Those of us who gave it our best ended up connected to each other. The folks who just showed up and expected to get something stopped showing up because they didn't get what they were looking for. They pretty much got what they gave!

Community requires a commitment to be there and a commitment to work at it until it happens. And when it does, it changes your life.

IN SUMMARY

JOANNE:

When I think of community, I think of a group of people who want to know me as well as I know myself — people who challenge my thinking, help me grow, and love me unconditionally. Community like that is incredibly freeing.

When Jesus encountered the woman at the well in John 4, He told her all about herself. At first, she was caught off guard and uneasy. But she soon went back to her town and told everyone to come and meet the man who knew all about her.

As believers, we have a great opportunity to use community to reach others with the gospel. As we participate in community, people on the outside will see that and want to be part of it. I encourage you to find community and to share that community with others.

∞

VOICE OF WISDOM

When Kevin and Mary McKee got married, they set out to follow Deuteronomy 24:5: "If a man has recently married, he must not be sent to war or have any other duty laid on him. For one year he is to be free to stay at home and bring happiness to the wife he has married" (NIV). Fortunately for Kevin and Mary, there were no wars when they got married.

Following are the collected comments gathered over a lunch we shared on their back deck over a couple of shrimp po' boys.

Mary: Kevin wanted to go to seminary, so we moved to Dallas from Louisiana. We knew seminary was going to be challenging, so we tried to take a year together before Kevin got started. In our first year of marriage we got involved in a class for young couples at our church. The class ended up breaking off from the rest of the church to do a church plant. Kevin and I had been really involved in ministry up to that point and we wanted to just "show up" for a while and not get too involved. After that, we started going to Fellowship Bible and met Steve and Darlene.

Joanne: Did this couple have a mentoring influence on your marriage?

Kevin: Before we were married we had couples that we admired, but after we got married I started thinking about being a husband and a dad. After we met Steve and Darlene, I remember being over at their house and watching Steve put his daughter to bed. Years later, she came by the church to show me her new car. We sat out

181

there for a while, and I was so struck by what a great kid she turned out to be. I still remember watching Steve put her to bed. It clued me in to the responsibilities and potential of being a father.

Mary: We've always had mentoring couples in our lives — people who we admired. We worked to find ways to be around them. Some were good friends. Others were not especially close, but we had plenty of opportunities to observe their marriages. We didn't really think about them as "mentors" but just as older friends.

We both wanted to be exposed to "aged" marriages — not just new ones. That's incredibly valuable. Having those older couples around gave us a visible goal. We would ask ourselves from time to time, "Is this something Walt and Dottie would do?"

We had other really close friends who got married about the same time we did. Shared experiences are so important. I remember we'd sit around and talk about things like what to do for our first Christmas — whose house we should go to. We would make decisions together and then sometimes suffer the consequences together. We were together in recovery from bad decisions!

Toben: Sounds like you have defined two kinds of community: "mentoring" friends and "peer" friends. What is it that differentiates community from being "just friends"?

Kevin: Putting God in the middle makes all the difference. Prayer is key. You don't all have to go to the same church. If you're sharing Christ, then you're on the path to community. If you're just sharing experiences, then who knows where you are?

Mary: We try to be Jesus to nonChristians 24-7. You have to be

182

on purpose to connect spiritually with your peer friends. Older couples tend to take the lead on spiritual things, and that makes it a little easier.

Joanne: How did you get started making these kinds of friendships?

Mary: We entertained a lot. That fostered community. We had everyone over — our single friends and our married friends. We fed some of our friends twice a week for the entire first year of our marriage. Let me add that not hanging out with your single friends after you get married makes them feel terrible. Single friends have to put up with you whining about married stuff, and married friends have to put up with their single friends appearing to be so self-centered. Deal with it, but don't abandon those relationships.

Kevin: We also taught Sunday school, and that was a good experience for us. Newly married couples have great opportunities for easy ministry that just takes an hour a week. It's a good way to get involved and to get to know people. Service is a great way to find community.

Toben: Seems like when some couples get married, they really focus on each other and have no interest in community or making friends, especially if they move into a new town. Why should newly married couples do the work of connecting with others?

Mary: You can't meet 100 percent of your mate's needs for fun, spirituality, or whatever. Hard times are going to come, and you are going to need the support that only others can provide. Maybe that's as simple as having a friend to go to lunch with who can give you some perspective.

I remember going out with a friend once and telling her, "Kevin has worked late the last four nights." I felt like he didn't love me anymore and that I was having to carry more of the burden than I wanted. She told me about a time in her marriage when her husband had been overseas for three months. That changed my perspective a little. Four nights of working late didn't seem like such a big deal.

Kevin: Familiarity breeds contempt. If you don't get out, you are going to drive each other crazy.

Joanne: I know that service is a big deal to you guys. What does that have to do with building community?

Kevin: Our marriages are collections of experiences. When you serve together you can debrief over lunch, and that creates a great connection between two people. The more you do together and with other people, the healthier your marriage will be. You have to cultivate yourself, apart from your spouse, so that you are both growing. And serving is a great way to grow.

Mary: Just showing up at church won't make it happen. It may be a place to start, but it doesn't happen spontaneously. It takes work. Any place you can give or serve will lead to community. You create community through service and submission.

Serve one another. Serve someone else. Live life together with other people. That makes it easier to bring others into community. Kevin and I try to avoid being exclusive. I've been excluded, and I know how much that can hurt. It kills groups and communities. You have to be open to having anyone get involved. I've heard some couples say, "We love these five couples so much that we don't want to let anyone else in to mess it up." As soon as you say that, your community is in jeopardy. Don't close your community but expand and divide it. And keep dividing. Variety is key, and if you don't share the community you've got, it will die.

Toben: Okay, give us a summary of your thoughts on community.

Kevin: In Mark 10:45 it says, "That is what the Son of Man has done: He came to serve, not to be served — and then to give away his life in exchange for many who are held hostage." When you give your life away, you experience true life — you share in Christ's life. If you do that in your marriage by opening your home and your lives, you will experience that true life and will be part of a dynamic community.

DISCUSSION QUESTIONS

- How would you define community?

- How much time and energy are you willing to commit to be part of a community?

- Have you ever been part of a community? Describe it.*

- What do you remember about your parents' friendships? How has that influenced your views of adult friendships?*

- Do you think real community must involve a spiritual component? Why, or why not?

- What are the benefits of community to you as an individual and as a couple?*

- If you're not in a community now, how might you go about finding or creating one?

- What qualities and characteristics do you look for in your friends? How is that similar to or different from what your spouse values?*

- Describe a couple you know whose marriage is a "lighthouse" to those around them.

- Is it important to you for your marriage to be a "lighthouse"? Why, or why not?

- Do you get more energy from being around other people or from being alone? How might that affect your view of community?

- How is community different from friendship?

- What are some needs you have that your partner doesn't meet? Are they things you need to work on together, or are they needs friends could meet for you? Which of your friends could meet those needs?*

- If you had an emergency, how many people could you call for help at 2 A.M.? Would they feel free to call you?

---

* *Questions ideal for journaling*

CHAPTER EIGHT

What You Believe

SPIRITUALITY AND MARRIAGE

TOBEN:

Joanne and I attended Presbyterian churches for most of the time when we were growing up, although both of our families had a brief stint in the Methodist church. We attended a Presbyterian college, and after we married we attended a nondenominational church just down the road.

We moved to Paris and went to services at the American Church a few times, moved back to Colorado and went back to the Presbyterian church, then tried the Episcopal church and a couple more nondenominational churches.

At times we have been very faithful participants, involved in Sunday school and small groups. We attended services every week and volunteered our time to help out with the high school group or some other ministry. Other times we hardly went to church at all, particularly right after we were married. We were finishing college and just couldn't get out the door Sunday mornings. To me, it wasn't a very big deal. But looking back, I think Joanne wrestled a bit with our lackadaisical attendance.

Joanne's family didn't miss church — ever. Even if they were on vacation, they would usually find a local church to worship at on Sundays. She remembers vacationing in Germany during junior high school and attending a German service. None of them spoke German — but they were there anyway!

Church was important to my parents as well. My dad was even an ordained minister for a time when I was very young. But as I got older, it seemed like church was optional. Most Sundays we'd get there, but if we didn't... so be it. And we certainly didn't go to church while on vacation.

As a result, Joanne and I had very different ideas about what church was for, how frequently we should go, and what would happen if we didn't go. We never really talked about it, but I think Joanne felt terrible that we were skipping church with some frequency.

Throughout our marriage, as we went through these cycles of attendance and absence, Joanne would generally be the one who felt compelled to get back to church. I'm sad to say that I was the one who resisted going. You may have strong feelings about the husband being the "spiritual head" in a marriage. Or you may have a less stringent opinion. Or it's possible you may not know what I'm talking about. But let me say this: Joanne has done more to keep our marriage spiritually on task than I have ever done.

After being married for six years and going through a hurtful experience at a church we'd been pretty active in, Joanne and I finally landed in a church that we both love. The point of all this is that the church represents a relationship that has had both positive and negative impacts on our lives. When we talk about our expectations of church or worship, we have the opportunity to challenge each other and build one another up in faith.

FIRST STEPS

What role did church play in your family as you grew up?

Hanna: Even before my parents were Christians, we went to church every week. We prayed over dinner, and I went to the youth group. But that's about it. It was more guilt-motivated until the family became believers.

Brian: We went to church out of habit more than anything else. I don't think it really influenced the rest of the week. I didn't see it influencing things within our family. My parents are very private about their faith, so it wasn't a community sort of a deal.

BUMPS IN THE ROAD

One of the things that can most directly impact our view of religion is whether we feel we have suffered some injury or injustice at the hands of the church. I've heard about people who were hurt in some way by a church they attended. One friend of mine has even gone so far as to say that he loves God but can't stand "church people." His dad is a pastor, and my friend suffered the slings and arrows that often accompany growing up in the fishbowl of church ministry.

Joanne and I have certainly been through ups and downs at churches — particularly one church we attended. When things were going right, we experienced huge amounts of joy and a sense of connectedness in that body. But when they started to go wrong, it was awful.

We had helped start a ministry for other young couples that was really taking off. We were seeing people involved in church who hadn't gone in years. Our small-group ministry had about twelve couples coming together weekly to study Scripture.

Unfortunately, we had some ministry goals and expectations that ran in a different direction from where the church was headed. We were trying to provide an on-ramp to further involvement in the church. The church expected couples to come in through the front doors of the church, and they viewed the young couples class as an off-ramp. Beyond that, because we were young and childless, we were viewed as a great labor pool for the church. They had a lot of expectations about our involvement in the nursery ministry and the parking lot ministry.

192

It was their way or the highway. And because we felt their way ran counter to the integrity of what we were doing, Joanne and I departed. We encouraged the other leadership couples to stay, thinking that maybe the conflict was somewhat personal and that someone else would be able to take the program effectively forward. For a couple of months, to their credit, a handful of those couples made the best of it, but in the end the church managed to run us all off.

This was incredibly painful for Joanne and me. We had invested two years of our lives in this ministry and saw it disappear almost overnight. We saw friends get hurt and disillusioned with the church as well. We all took a few months off, not attending services anywhere. But before long we had the sense that God desired for us to be in the church and, one by one, we all got involved in new churches.

Even though it can be hard, I'm convinced that God wants us to be involved in the church and to worship corporately.

In His grace, God has used the leadership experiences that each of us gained in that ministry to go on to minister in other churches. Lisa leads the drama ministry at her church. Steve plays the drums in a worship band at his church. Steve and Michelle lead a small-group Bible study and teach children's Sunday school at their church. And Joanne and I helped start a new Gen X ministry at the church we used to attend. God can take bad situations and produce good results, and that's what He did for each of us in His own time and in His own way.

THE BODY OF CHRIST

*J*OANNE:

The New Testament is full of examples of church. From Antioch (see Acts 13:1) to Joppa (see Acts 9:42), we find individual churches filled with believers. The church played an integral role in the growth of Christianity.

So what makes church so important? As we discussed in the chapter on community, the church presents true community to the world at large. As people see how the church functions and cares for the people within it, they are drawn to learn more about what makes the church community so different.

But we should be attending church for other reasons too. First and foremost, we should go because we are commanded to do so: "Let's see how inventive we can be in encouraging love and helping out, not avoiding worshiping together as some do but spurring each other on, especially as we see the big Day approaching" (Hebrews 10:24-25).

It couldn't be stated more clearly — we are to worship together.

As Toben said, we've been off and on with our church attendance since we were married. Like anything else in life, when we miss a week or two of church, it's all the harder to get back into the habit of regular attendance. Especially since Audrey was born, we've had a difficult time getting to church — and an easy time coming up with reasons for our absence: "She doesn't like the nursery." "It's right in the middle of nap time." (The funny thing about writing this book has been how often I've written something and been struck with conviction for our own marriage. This is one of those times!)

194

While it's not possible to attend church sometimes, for the most part I'm learning that there's really no excuse. Nap time or not! After all, even Jesus went to church — and He was God: "He came to Nazareth where he had been reared. As he always did on the Sabbath, he went to the meeting place" (Luke 4:16).

Okay, but what about the fact that the church isn't a building, but people? True. In 1 Corinthians 3:16, Paul wrote, "You realize, don't you, that you are the temple of God, and God himself is present in you?"

And what about when Jesus said this: "And when two or three of you are together because of me, you can be sure that I'll be there" (Matthew 18:20)? Hey! A marriage is two people. Okay, Jesus is present and — voilà — instant church!

I know it sounds a little silly, but we've actually used that logic a time or two to justify sleeping in on Sunday morning. And that's part of the problem. There are three important words in what Jesus says: *"because of me."*

If you and your spouse are together for the purpose of Christ — to worship and praise Him together — that is the body of Christ, and, I believe, that is church. But it's still not ideal. Why not? Because it takes more than two parts to make a whole body.

In 1 Corinthians 12, Paul likens the body of Christ to a human body:

> *You can easily enough see how this kind of thing works by looking no further than your own body. Your body has many parts — limbs, organs, cells — but no matter how many parts you can name, you're still one body. It's exactly the same with Christ. . . .*
>
> *The way God designed our bodies is a model for understanding our lives together as a church: every part dependent on every other part, the parts we mention and the parts we don't, the parts we see and the parts we don't. If one part hurts, every other part is involved in the hurt, and in the healing. If one part flourishes, every other part enters into the exuberance.*
>
> *You are Christ's body — that's who you are! You must never forget this. Only as you accept your part of that body does your "part" mean anything (verses 12, 25-27).*

195

As a believer, you are part of the body of Christ. And your place is with all the other parts of that body. So now that you're headed for church, how do you decide which one to attend?

A Question of Style

*T*OBEN:

Organ music and a choir in robes, or a praise-and-worship band complete with electric guitars and drums? An old-fashioned fire-and-brimstone preacher who teaches exegetically, or a pastor who relates Scripture to life while always remaining sensitive to the "seekers" in attendance? Finding a church that "fits" can be a real challenge for couples who have grown up in different churches or denominations.

Our church backgrounds are fairly similar. We were familiar with Sunday school, communion about once a month, and hymns. But even with our similar backgrounds, we respond to and look for different things in a church service. Joanne loves hymns and a formal service. I like a good band and contemporary music.

For others, finding a church home where both people feel comfortable can be more difficult than deciding which musical style to go with. We recently met a couple about to be married. He was raised in the Catholic Church and has only recently accepted Christ as his personal savior. She was raised in an evangelical church and made a decision to accept Christ when she was a child. Needless to say, they're starting at ground zero as they try to decide where to plug in. Some liturgical churches feel pretty normal to him; they feel stuffy to her and void of the praise and worship she's used to. To him, the churches that she likes seem too laid back and don't hold the same sense of awe and mystery that he wants to experience in worship. Eventually, they will find a church that works well for both of them. But until then, it's critical that they keep talking about what is working and not working for them in the churches they attend.

If you're in this position, it might provide some insight for you to attend together the churches that you grew up in. That way each of you can see firsthand what feels "right" to your spouse. If that's not possible, at least visit several churches when looking for a church home. Try churches with different worship styles and music styles, and spend time talking about what you liked about each one. Consider meeting the leadership in the church — they can answer any questions you may have and provide additional insight into the church.

FIRST STEPS

What do you look for in a church home?

Hanna: I think both of us really want to be involved in the church we go to. As students, we liked our church but didn't have time to be involved as much. We really want to make friends of all different ages and be able to serve in the church.

Brian: I'd agree with that. Having come from a church that never presented itself as terribly genuine, I'm looking for a church that is more authentic. I think I've always had difficulty believing that a huge church can be authentic, so I think I'm wanting a smaller church — one that's about people rather than numbers.

THE "ONE ANOTHERS"

There's so much more to spirituality in your marriage than just church. The New Testament is full of what many people call the "one anothers." These verses about how we should treat other people are essential for learning about community. But I think that in marriage — in the community of two — we find the greatest opportunity to learn how to love another person. When we make the "one anothers" a practice in our marriages, we're better equipped to reach out to others.

So what's included in the "one anothers"? Here's a short list:

- "Take this most seriously: A yes on earth is yes in heaven; a no on earth is no in heaven. What you say to one another is eternal. I mean this." (Matthew 18:18)
- "Let me give you a new command: Love one another. In the same way I loved you, you love one another." (John 13:34)
- "So reach out and welcome one another to God's glory. Jesus did it; now *you* do it!" (Romans 15:7)
- "I'll put it as urgently as I can: You *must* get along with each other. You must learn to be considerate of one another, cultivating a life in common." (1 Corinthians 1:10)
- "So, my friends, when you come together to the Lord's Table, be reverent and courteous with one another." (1 Corinthians 11:33)
- "Greet one another with a holy embrace." (2 Corinthians 13:12)
- "It is absolutely clear that God has called you to a free life. Just make sure that you don't use this freedom as an excuse to do whatever you want to do and destroy your freedom. Rather, use your freedom to serve one another in love; that's how freedom grows." (Galatians 5:13)
- "Be gentle with one another, sensitive. Forgive one another as quickly and thoroughly as God in Christ forgave you." (Ephesians 4:32)

- "Out of respect for Christ, be courteously reverent to one another." (Ephesians 5:21)
- "Don't lie to one another. You're done with that old life. It's like a filthy set of ill-fitting clothes you've stripped off and put in the fire." (Colossians 3:9)
- "Let the Word of Christ — the Message — have the run of the house. Give it plenty of room in your lives. Instruct and direct one another using good common sense. And sing, sing your hearts out to God!" (Colossians 3:16)
- "Regarding life together and getting along with each other, you don't need me to tell you what to do. You're *God*-taught in these matters. Just love one another!" (1 Thessalonians 4:9)
- "So reassure one another with these words." (1 Thessalonians 4:18)
- "So speak encouraging words to one another. Build up hope so you'll all be together in this, no one left out, no one left behind. I know you're already doing this; just keep on doing it." (1 Thessalonians 5:11)
- "Now that you've cleaned up your lives by following the truth, love one another as if your lives depended on it." (1 Peter 1:22)
- "No one has seen God, ever. But if we love one another, God dwells deeply within us, and his love becomes complete in us — perfect love!" (1 John 4:12)

Loving one another, being honest with one another, getting along with one another, reassuring one another, serving one another, encouraging one another, forgiving one another, being considerate of one another — just think what your marriage could be like if you consistently practiced all of these things!

Personally, I'd suggest starting with the holy embrace — or the holy kiss, as some other versions of the Bible translate it!

*T*OBEN:

It's so easy to forget these "one anothers" — especially when things aren't going well. For me, just rereading this list gives me a sense of hope and purpose in wanting to love and serve Joanne. Maybe I'll print these out and carry them around in my daily calendar so that I'm constantly reminded of how I am to relate to her.

SHARED SPIRITUALITY 101

*J*OANNE:

One of the best examples my parents set for me is one of prayer. When I was a child, we regularly prayed together as a family and alone with Mom and Dad before going to sleep each night. As I got older, we didn't pray as much as a family. But as a couple, Mom and Dad kept it up. I know that even today, each morning they pray together before going their separate ways. Each day of the week is filled with people they faithfully remember in prayer.

Unfortunately, as great as their example has been and still is, Toben and I don't pray together very often. I'm not sure why this is. I want to pray together, and I think Toben does too. Perhaps it's a matter of finding the time — making the time — and deciding that prayer is something we will do.

On my own, I pray throughout the day. My requests aren't always eloquent, but they're honest, and I never seem to have a lack of words to express my feelings of anxiousness, gratitude, or desire to God. Praying aloud, however, is another matter. Despite growing up in a Christian family, being an active leader in my high school youth group, and attending a Christian college and numerous Bible studies, I sometimes feel tongue-tied and even foolish when I pray aloud.

In my heart, I know my feelings of inadequacy don't really matter. And I know that prayer, like anything, gets easier the more you do it. After all, we're commanded in Scripture to pray for each other. And in marriage, I think that means praying together as well as alone.

James wrote this to the church: "Make this your common practice: Confess your sins to each other and pray for each other so that you can live together whole and healed" (James 5:16). If this kind of confession and prayer is good for the church body as a whole, it must also be good for the community of marriage.

One friend who's been married for sixteen years told us that she and her husband have prayed together on and off throughout their marriage. Then she said something that really struck me: "These days we don't pray together except at meals and occasional instances. I find praying together is a very intimate thing — almost too intimate to be comfortable. You have to be so honest with God and with your spouse that there's no room for hiding whatsoever."

Another friend, Rebecca, and her husband have made prayer part of their marriage from the beginning. "We pray together because we think it keeps our relationship together with God. The difficulty," she said, "is finding the time. It must be a priority."

Like prayer, Bible reading is a point of connection for shared spirituality. One friend who has been married for almost twenty years said

that Bible reading has been an integral part of his and his wife's spirituality. "One key factor in our spiritual lives has been a strong commitment
to daily Bible reading together," he said. "Sometimes we let it slide, but
overall we try hard to stick with it. We do the kind of Bible reading each
of us was doing before we got married — that made it easy and natural
to just keep doing together what we'd done separately before."

He went on to say that they really encourage each other's spirituality through continuing conversation. "We talk about [what] we read
this morning, about Sunday's sermon, about this meeting at church —
and force ourselves to look at our own spiritual qualities. We greatly
value time in the morning for a cup of coffee right before or after our
Bible reading, as well as a debriefing cup at the end of the day."

202

FIRST STEPS

Do you pray together?

Hanna: Yes. I think that our prayer comes out of need. When I was
going through a hard time at work, we knew that we didn't have
the strength to go through it alone. We knew that we needed
God to meet us and intervene. As far as reaching out with
prayer, we pray for our families, but we're not intentional about
praying for specific things. We're good about praying for the
class-one important things, but not so much for the class-two
important things.

Brian: I was in some need when we first started dating, and I didn't have
a choice. I had to pray at that point and Hanna was there, so we
prayed together.

Hanna: I'd never met anyone before Brian who could communicate with me on such deep levels. We needed guidance for how to deal with those big issues we talked about — from our personal lives to our own relationship with each other. So we looked to God for that guidance.

SPIRITUAL LEADERSHIP

Something that has surprised me as I've talked to other women about spirituality and marriage has been the desire for our husbands to initiate prayer and quiet time together. The topic of leadership in marriage is one that can cause disagreement. But as a couple, it's important to discuss your expectations about it.

We weren't really sure if we should include something on spiritual leadership in this book and even debated about taking it out. But we've found that it's a discussion we've had with newly married couples more often than not. The topic is one that couples struggle with, and so we decided to address it briefly here.

My friend Lisa told me that she struggles with the idea of shared spirituality. "We used to pray together before meals and before going to bed, but because of our schedules we have slacked off. We've never really studied the Bible together or prayed as part of a regular time alone with God," she said. "And it's difficult to start now after being married almost four years. We're both appallingly lax in our own private times with God. My husband is a private person — especially when it comes to his spiritual life. But deep down I want him to be the spiritual head of the house."

So what does it look like to be the spiritual head of the house?

Part of it is initiation, Lisa said. She wants her husband to take the lead in prayer and Bible study. "I consider myself a feminist, yet I still long for the image of man as protector," she said. "I want my husband to create an environment of unity before God, a haven I can rest in.

"Being the head doesn't mean being better or higher," Lisa went on to say. "It's servant leadership — and that's hard."

When I asked a friend who's been married for almost thirty years about this, she stressed the importance of stating what she wants. "We tried at different times to have prayer and devotions together, but my perfectionism got in the way of enjoying whatever level my husband could supply," Kathy said. "I wanted to spend an hour together, but he just doesn't enjoy studying with me."

She went on to say, "I got tired of always having to initiate, thinking that 'leadership' meant he would. But he just doesn't think of it, so now I'm content to initiate prayer. He's had a weird work schedule in the past, but just this week he started working day shifts. We've already begun praying together, and I have new freedom to be satisfied with however he leads."

A BIBLICAL MODEL FOR LEADERSHIP IN MARRIAGE

*T*OBEN:

Before I give my two cents about leadership, let's look at what the Bible has to say about it. I particularly like the way *The Message* translates this passage in Ephesians:

Out of respect for Christ, be courteously reverent to one another.

Wives, understand and support your husbands in ways that show your support for Christ. The husband provides leadership to his wife the way Christ does to his church, not by domineering but by cherishing. So just as the church submits to Christ as he exercises such leadership, wives should likewise submit to their husbands.

Husbands, go all out in your love for your wives, exactly as Christ did for the church — a love marked by giving, not getting. Christ's love makes the church whole. His words evoke her beauty. Everything he does and says is designed to bring the best out of her, dressing her in dazzling white silk, radiant with holiness. And that is how husbands ought to love their wives. They're really doing themselves a favor — since they're already "one" in marriage.

No one abuses his own body, does he? No, he feeds and pampers it. That's how Christ treats us, the church, since we are part of his body. And this is why a man leaves father and mother and cherishes his wife. No longer two, they become "one flesh." This is a huge mystery, and I don't pretend to understand it all. What is clearest to me is the way Christ treats the church. And this provides a good picture of how each husband is to treat his wife, loving himself in loving her, and how each wife is to honor her husband. (5:21-33)

It was the best small-group meeting we had ever had, and in some ways it was also the worst. Our group had been meeting together for some time, and we were talking about marriage. We'd covered a lot of the topics included in this book, but somehow we always shied away from discussing leadership. I think we knew that it was potentially explosive, but we'd built up a lot of trust with each other over the months, so we decided to try it.

The night that we looked at the passage above, there were some tears as couples honestly grappled with what it might mean to live out these verses. Depending on how each couple had wrestled with them and what had been modeled to them growing up, they either brought confirmation or confusion.

At least two couples in our group had pretty traditional views of "headship." They talked things over, but in the end, the husband made the decision. At least two other couples shared the opinion that all decisions had to be mutually agreed upon and that if they couldn't be like-minded on the decision, then it didn't get made until they talked it through and ended up at the same place. The fifth couple was down-right offended by the passage.

For our friends Doug and Lisa, this passage brought a great deal of freedom. Lisa longed for Doug to be the spiritual head of their relationship and found a great deal of comfort in knowing that he would make the difficult decisions that they faced. Because of that, Doug felt supported and empowered by Lisa and made decisions that were honoring to her.

One woman in the group stated plainly that she didn't get married so a man could tell her what to do. He was "not the boss of her" and any decision he made that she didn't like, well, look out! "Who am I to tell her what to do?" summed up her husband's view. I think they might have missed the point of the passage.

More than the passage itself, it seemed like the couples in our group were more influenced by the ways their parents had lived out these verses. The two couples who had given it the most thought and had spent the most time talking about it came from divorced families. They didn't have a model to fall back on, so they had to start from scratch and validate what they did through Scripture.

We can't deny or easily overcome what was modeled to us growing up. But at the same time, we can't deny that as Christians, the Bible is the blueprint for everything we do. The couples who struggled most with this passage had parents who didn't live it out. Because of that, it ran counter to their experience and made it difficult for them to accept and even more difficult for them to implement.

If you had a great childhood and look fondly on your parents, it's hard to acknowledge that maybe the way they did things wasn't the best or right way. After all, if you love them and they love each other, then how can the way they choose to live be wrong? Scripture refers to the sins of a father being revisited on his children (see Exodus 34:7). Sometimes those sins are revisited because it's so easy to go with what was modeled — right or wrong.

With leadership, like everything else in marriage, it is important to know why you do what you do. When the going gets tough, if you don't know why your husband made a particular decision — especially one you disagree with — you may say to yourself, "Up to this point I've been okay going along with him. But now that he has obviously gone insane, I don't have to go along with this, right?" But that kind of attitude won't make your relationship stronger.

Communication seems to be key. If you are clear about the why, then these situations can be avoided. I'm not here to interpret Ephesians 5 for you and tell you how to view leadership in your marriage. But I am here to tell you that your marriage can only benefit from taking the time to get beyond what was modeled to you to what is prescribed in the Bible — and you need to agree on what that is. Perhaps you'll decide to talk about this topic with older couples or the pastor at your church; in addition to the Scriptures themselves, you may want to read books that others recommend about spiritual leadership in marriage.

Finally, let me add this as a word of encouragement: I can't recall a time when Joanne and I were really at odds over a big decision that had to be made. A few years ago, I was offered a great job on the East Coast. Taking the job would have meant leaving our friends and family, a town that we know and love, and our church. As we considered the decision both independently and together, we often prayed that we would come to the same decision. Joanne made it clear from the outset that if I felt called to the church, then we would pack up and go. That would be that.

I know that she wrestled with the implications of that move, as did I. But on the same day at practically the same time we both knew that we weren't called to go. I came home from work and said, "I think we're supposed to stay here." She said she felt the same thing. If I had gone the other way, I have no doubt that Joanne would have supported the decision 100 percent, but God honored our prayer that we be like-minded.

Maybe you'll face very few decisions where you're at odds. I sincerely hope that will be the case. But at some point it will happen, so take the time to figure out how you're going to handle it before you get there.

IN SUMMARY

JOANNE:

Along with sex, our shared spirituality has the potential to be one of the most intimate — if not the most intimate — facets of our marriage. It encompasses the relationship we have with each other and the relationship we have with God. And God is as central to our marriage as our spouse is. In Ecclesiastes 4:12, Solomon wrote that a cord of three strands is not easily broken. With God as an integral part of marriage, marriage becomes stronger.

A shared spirituality comes more easily for some couples than it does for others. For those who spend time together in prayer and Bible reading, the key seems to be that they make it a priority. My parents always told me that love isn't a feeling, but a choice. It's the same with our faith. We may not feel like spending time together with God, but as we make the choice to do so, the feelings will follow.

Over and over again, our relationship with Christ is compared to marriage. He is the bridegroom; the church is the bride. Marriage is important to God, and He wants us to build strong marriages based on Him.

VOICE OF WISDOM

—Original Message—

From: Toben Heim

Sent: Monday, August 23

To: Kathy@navpress

Subject: Let's begin to dialogue

Kathy,

Joanne and I have admired your marriage and the way you and Bob have made God central, so we thought you would have some great thoughts on this topic. Let me pose a couple of questions. When you respond, I may get back to you with a couple more as your comments spur additional thoughts.

1. A lot of times, young couples try to develop their married spirituality by reading the Bible together, praying together, and going to church on Sundays. Are there other ways to deepen your spirituality as a couple?

2. I've heard it said to almost every couple about to get married that, as they grow closer to God, they will grow closer to one another. Has that proved true in your marriage? How have you seen it happen?

3. Is there anything you did early on in your marriage that you would do differently if you had it to do over again?

4. What's the best advice you could offer a couple about to be married who really wants to grow in their relationship with God?

Let's start there and see where it leads us.

Toben

—Original Message—

From: Kathy Blume
Sent: Monday, August 30
To: Toben@navpress
Subject: Re: Let's begin to dialogue

Toben,

I've printed out your questions, and they are in front of me. I'll give you some input to the questions you asked in the order you asked them. We can go from there.

1. Reading the Bible, praying together, and going to church are all very good things and should basically be established during your dating time before marriage. But these three things aren't guarantees for a good marriage. You won't necessarily grow in spirituality because you do them.

When I look around at the church today, I see pews full of couples who probably think everything is just fine because they are doing these things. But it needs to go much deeper. We need to be the vehicle of grace in the lives of others, including the life of our spouse.

Let me offer a word of caution here. Please don't take this as a sexist remark but as an observation I've gained in my years of counseling women. Very often a woman may seem to be more spiritual than her husband because women have a natural bent toward relationships. Beyond that, men and women are raised differently. Consequently, many husbands will read the Bible and pray with their wives, but they are not really growing in their relationship with their wives and with God. Often, a wife might intimidate her husband with her "spiritual verbiage." And other times a husband may resent his wife's spiritual leadership in their marriage, especially if he comes from a home with a controlling mother and a weak father and looks with resentment on the way he saw them relate to one another.

So many women will say to me, "I don't know what happened. We started out reading the Bible together and praying together, but we don't do it anymore because now my husband is too tired or else he never initiates anything spiritual and I am tired of doing it." I think oftentimes, men do something because their wives want them to do it—not because they want to do it. It becomes behavior without intimacy, and it doesn't work.

The secret to developing a spiritual life together is realizing that our spiritual lives aren't separate from the rest of our marriage. Every part of marriage affects every other part. For Bob and me, the intimacy came when we began to spend time together connecting through the mundane. By that I mean that we got to a point where we were spending time alone together connecting through everyday things. The more we did that, the more our spiritual lives were woven together. As we reviewed the mundane events of our day, we began asking each other how God used the other that day. And we began praying about those mundane things, which expanded to praying for each other and for our family.

For me, the real key was realizing that God was more concerned with Bob's heart than I was. That was a real wake-up call! I remember one day Bob came home and told me to sit down. He then recited an entire chapter of the Bible to me. I was amazed and couldn't believe he'd had the time to do it—that he'd made the time to do it! And I realized that just because I didn't see Bob doing things to deepen his spiritual life didn't mean he wasn't. But it was only as we stepped back and entered into the mundane that he was comfortable sharing those things together with me.

2. Growing closer to God will ultimately draw you closer to each other. That is true. But here again, a word of caution: Intimacy involves conflict, or dying to self, on a daily basis—not being naïve about the other person. Hope is found when you accept one another. Love well and enter conflict for the other knowing God is on your side. God is pursuing your spouse and often it is through conflict.

In conflict, it's important to decide what hill is worth dying on. In our marriage, one of us is very black and white, and the other sees more shades of gray. As a result, the one who sees things in black and white tends to think that every hill is worth dying on! We've had to learn how to discern when it's appropriate to point out sin for each other and when it's best to be the face of God for the other through encouragement. Usually pain is involved in these things.

Do you suffer comfortably with your mate? Jesus was conformed to the image of His Father through His sufferings. Are you willing to suffer well with your mate? Growing deeper in the Lord and desiring to be more like Him will cause you and your spouse to flush things out of your life that may not be pretty. Repentance and forgiveness should be your traveling companions.

By suffering with your mate, I mean understanding where your spouse's pain is. Our marriage began in pain. This is the second marriage for each of us, and while our marriage was a happy event, it was surrounded by pain. Bob was grieving for his first wife, whom he lost to cancer. I was grieving for my divorce. And our teenagers were all grieving over the loss of one of their parents.

Recently, we've faced pain again. At age sixty, we were really looking ahead to a future of retirement, but Bob lost his job and we're facing a change in ministry instead. It's brought out insecurity in me and made Bob feel incompetent. He's not, but I need to let him work through that pain as he learns to view the last six years at his job not as a waste, but as training for a new phase of ministry. He doesn't understand my insecurity, but he's heard my heart and hasn't tried to change my mind about my feelings. We've grown closer to God and each other by clinging together and believing in God's sovereignty through this.

I know God is pursuing my husband and that the battle is not mine. This gives me much peace and joy as I watch God put all the pieces together. I can love my husband well, give him my heart, pray for him, encourage him, bless him. Then we will grow closer to God and to each other.

3. If I could turn the clock back and do some things differently, I would. I'd be more relaxed and let God be God. I'd stop trying to make my husband into the spiritual giant I wanted. I'd be more aware of the

manifestation of a deepening walk with the Lord through his actions and the way he treated me and others, instead of how much he read his Bible. I was too legalistic.

I used subtle spiritual manipulation to try to force Bob to be that spiritual giant. I dropped hints, saying things like, "I just finished reading through the Bible again" or "I prayed for two hours today." Those things weren't wrong for me to do, but what I meant in telling Bob those things was, "What have you done lately?"

I stopped trying to be God in Bob's life because I felt that God wanted me to stop. And because it wasn't working (if it had, I'd probably still be doing it!). I sensed God telling me to back off, to realize that I didn't need to keep Bob going. Like I said before, God cares more about my husband's heart than I do. I realized that I was causing him shame through my manipulation. He withdrew and did things only because I wanted him to. Those things didn't invite Bob to share his spiritual journey with me. That's when I learned to share the mundane with him.

But I have learned—and what freedom that has brought! A deeper intimacy has developed with the Lord and with each other. We love to minister together. Our gifts are different, our personalities are different, but our hearts are the same.

4. Couples have to establish their own individual commitment to Christ. Sometimes in marriage we assume that our spouses want us to be a part of their spiritual life, and that's not always true. For many people, their relationship with Christ is a very personal thing that they may not let many people into. So couples have to talk about how spirituality is going to be a part of their relationship—before they get

married. That's the thing that will lead to true and abiding intimacy.

The assumption here is that because we met in a church situation, our spiritual life together is already taken care of—without any planning or conversation. But we have to talk about it! Couples are going to be coming from two different ways of thinking, church backgrounds, families of origin, and so on. They have to set ground rules and goals concerning where they want to go and how they're going to get there. Most couples are intentional about their financial goals, career goals, and family goals but then just expect the spiritual side to happen. It won't. And everything else needs to revolve around that spiritual relationship if things are going to work. You have to let God in on all your decisions. Develop time together with the Lord. Share your heart with the Lord and with each other.

Setting spiritual goals is exciting because as you reach them, you get to create new ones. Just because a quiet time together over breakfast is working now doesn't mean you're locked into it for the rest of your life. Part of spiritual goals is understanding the season of your life.

When we first got married, our life was filled with teenage boys. So one of our spiritual goals was to intentionally be part of our sons' spiritual lives. We put a rec room in the basement, encouraged our kids to invite their friends over, always made plenty of food, and spent time with them and their friends—bringing spirituality into their everyday lives through conversation, hospitality, or a word of encouragement. And at least one of our sons' friends became a Christian through that contact with our family and is now in full-time ministry.

Through the different seasons of our lives, our spiritual goals have included fasting one day a week together, reading a devotional book

216

together, and participating in spiritual retreats. As we've matured and gone through the years, we've experienced a deeper intimacy through each season. We've become more relaxed together and love just spending time together with God.

Thanks for asking. It was good to remind myself of these things!

Kathy

DISCUSSION QUESTIONS

• What is your religious background?

• What role did religion play in your family when you were growing up?*

• How would you define spirituality?*

• Describe the church you grew up in.

• Is church going to be part of your marriage? How?*

• What kind of church would you like to attend? What about your partner?

• Do you plan to spend time together in prayer? When?

• Describe your quiet time.

• Do you plan to have devotions or quiet times together? How? When?

• Talk about headship (or leadership) and submission. What do those terms mean to you? Are they positive or negative concepts?*

• How did you become a believer? Have you thought about your testimony?*

• Read Ephesians 5 together and talk about how to apply this passage to your marriage.

---

* *Questions ideal for journaling*

Notes

CHAPTER ONE

1. Kathy Collard Miller and D. Larry Miller, *When the Honeymoon's Over: Building a Real-Life Marriage* (Wheaton, Ill.: Harold Shaw, 1997), p. 54.
2. Jack and Carole Mayhall, *Marriage Takes More Than Love* (Colorado Springs, Colo.: NavPress, 1996), p. 57.

CHAPTER TWO

1. Kathy Collard Miller and D. Larry Miller, *When the Honeymoon's Over: Building a Real-Life Marriage* (Wheaton, Ill.: Harold Shaw, 1997), p. 41.
2. See Dr. Gary Chapman, *The Five Love Languages: How to Express Heartfelt Commitment to Your Mate* (Chicago: Northfield Press, 1992).
3. Jack and Carole Mayhall, *Marriage Takes More Than Love* (Colorado Springs, Colo.: NavPress, 1996), p. 114.
4. Miller and Miller, pp. 103-104.

CHAPTER THREE

1. Jan Karon, *Out to Canaan* (New York: Viking/Penguin, 1997), p. 184.
2. Adapted from Jack and Carole Mayhall, *Marriage Takes More Than Love* (Colorado Springs, Colo.: NavPress, 1996), pp. 103-107.

3. Betty Malz, *Making Your Husband Feel Loved* (Lake Mary, Fla.: Creation House, 1990), p. 172.

CHAPTER FIVE

1. Kathy Collard Miller and D. Larry Miller, *When the Honeymoon's Over: Building a Real-Life Marriage* (Wheaton, Ill.: Harold Shaw, 1997), p. 101.

CHAPTER SIX

1. Kathy Collard Miller and D. Larry Miller, *When the Honeymoon's Over: Building a Real-Life Marriage* (Wheaton, Ill.: Harold Shaw, 1997), p. 55.
2. Jack and Carole Mayhall, *Marriage Takes More Than Love* (Colorado Springs, Colo.: NavPress, 1996), p. 56.
3. Jan Karon, *These High, Green Hills* (New York: Viking/Penguin, 1996), pp. 120-121.
4. The compilation is *Help Lord, I'm Sinking!* (Colorado Springs, Colo.: NavPress, 1997).

CHAPTER SEVEN

1. Faith Popcorn, *The Popcorn Report: Faith Popcorn on the Future of Your Company, Your World, Your Life* (New York: Doubleday, 1991), p. 28.

Afterword

We love being married and are excited for you as you begin your life together. We hope you have as much fun being married as we have.

> So this is my prayer: that your love will flourish and that you will not only love much but well. Learn to love appropriately. You need to use your head and test your feelings so that your love is sincere and intelligent, not senti-mental gush. Live a lover's life, circumspect and exemplary, a life Jesus will be proud of: bountiful in fruits from the soul, making Jesus Christ attrac-tive to all, getting everyone involved in the glory and praise of God. (Philippians 1:9-11)

Resources

Chapter One: Where You Come From—Family History

- *The New Birth Order Book* by Kevin Leman (Revell) explains how your birth order (firstborn, middle child, youngest, only child, and so on) affects your personality and the way you react to different situations. This is a great book to read to understand both yourself and your spouse a little better.

- In their book *When the Honeymoon's Over: Building a Real-Life Marriage* (Shaw), Larry and Kathy Miller include a great list of things to talk about in terms of what's important to each of you in your marriage. From keeping a clean house and going on dates regularly to sleeping in and deciding who fixes things when they break, they encourage you to rank the importance of a variety of things and talk about why they're important or unimportant to you.

- *Boundaries* by Dr. Henry Cloud and Dr. John Townsend (Zondervan) is a thorough guide to understanding boundaries and how they affect our lives. There is a companion workbook available. The same authors have also written a new book, *Boundaries in Marriage,* that talks about how to set boundaries with your spouse.

- *The Book of Us: A Journal of Your Love Story in 150 Questions* by David and Kate Marshall (Hyperion) is a great way to record your story. Divided into several sections, the book asks questions from different periods of your life together and provides spaces to record your answers.

- *www.buildingrelationships.com,* the website of Life Innovations, Inc., provides information about the PREPARE/ENRICH program, a widely used resource designed to help engaged and married couples identify their individual strengths and growth areas in the major issues this book has covered. Trained counselors administer an inventory and offer help in interpreting and working through areas of conflict. The website enables you to search for a counselor in your area.

CHAPTER TWO: HOW YOU RELATE — COMMUNICATION

- *When the Honeymoon's Over: Building a Real-Life Marriage* by Larry and Kathy Miller (Shaw) covers a lot of marriage issues in a fun way. Underlying everything they say — about expectations, sex, serving and leading, and more — is the importance of good communication with your spouse. They define some different temperaments, giving couples a good place to start discussing their similarities and differences — and how they complement each other.

- *Words That Hurt, Words That Heal* by Carole Mayhall (NavPress) examines the power our words have to harm or heal other people. I (Joanne) found this book especially challenging and encouraging as I realized that I'm not the only one who struggles with this issue and that God can change my heart — and the words that come from it.

- *Marriage Takes More Than Love* by Jack and Carole Mayhall (NavPress) is one of my (Joanne's) favorite books about marriage. The biggest section in this book is about communication and the choices we make to communicate openly, honestly, and lovingly with our spouses. This book also has a huge section at the back filled with discussion questions designed to get couples talking about their relationship and voicing their expectations about all kinds of subjects.

- *The Five Love Languages: How to Express Heartfelt Commitment to Your Mate* by Dr. Gary Chapman (Northfield Press) describes the whole concept of love language in greater detail than we've touched on here.

CHAPTER THREE: HOW YOU RESOLVE CONFLICT — FIGHTING FAIRLY

- *The Marriage Mender: A Couple's Guide to Staying Together* by Tom Whiteman and Tom Bartlett (NavPress) is a great resource for learning to deal with conflict in your marriage. Even if you haven't come up against any big issues so far, this is a wonderful guide that will equip you to manage conflict effectively.

- *Uncommon Graces* by John Vawter (NavPress) identifies seven "graces" that are increasingly rare in our society today. From gentleness and candor to mercy and repentance, this book gives guidance on showing grace to a hostile world. While much of the book addresses our relationship with the world at large, its message is ideal for marriage as well.

CHAPTER FOUR: HOW YOU SPEND — FINANCES

- Larry Burkett is one of the most well-known and respected Christian authors on the subject of money. His books include the following: *The Complete Guide to Managing Your Money; The Family Budget Workbook; Debt-Free Living: How to Get Out of Debt and Stay Out;* and *Women Leaving the Workplace: How to Make the Transition from Work to Home* (Moody).

- Financial consultants aren't available only to people with a lot of money. There are a number of services that are available in most cities — and some for free. A financial consultant can help you come up with a budget and create a plan to save money. They also can offer perspective on any money issues you may be facing.

- Consumer credit counseling is also available to help you get out of debt. Search the Internet for help (not for more loans!).

- The book of Proverbs has a lot of good advice about money. Take a month to read Proverbs (one chapter each day) and discuss what you learn about money.

$\mathscr{C}$HAPTER $\mathscr{F}$IVE: WHAT YOU EXPECT — SEX

- *Intimate Issues* by Linda Dillow and Lorraine Pintus (WaterBrook) is by far the best book I (Joanne) have read about sex. The authors asked one thousand women to tell them their most common questions about sex and chose the twenty-one most-asked questions as the chapters for the book. It examines such issues as how to be godly and sensuous, heal past sexual sin, spice up your sex life, and much more. Reading this book feels a lot like sitting down and having a good heart-to-heart chat with a close friend.

- *The Act of Marriage* by Tim and Beverly LaHaye (Zondervan) is a thorough and clear explanation of sex and how to do it. It is a frank and open explanation of how our bodies work, and it provides basic information on sexual technique. At times it is a little old-fashioned (the authors conclude that women know more about how a sewing machine works than their own bodies and that most women stay home while men work), but if you can get past that, the information can be helpful.

- The Song of Songs, or Song of Solomon as it's called in some Bible translations, is God's book about sex. As the creator of sex, God thinks it's important and included this racy book in the Bible. Filled with imagery and romance, this book describes sex as God created it. Try reading it in *The Message,* published by NavPress.

Chapter Six: How You Celebrate — For Better or Worse

• The book of Psalms is a great example of thanking God in the midst of difficult circumstances. Psalms is also a great example of the joy that comes from praising God. Consider reading Psalms together as devotions. You can read through the entire book in a month by reading just five psalms a day. On the first day of the month, read Psalm 1, 31, 61, 91, and 121. On the second day, read Psalm 2, 32, 62, 92, and 122. And so on. We love reading Psalms from *The Message*.

• As you begin your own celebrations and traditions, keep an eye out for fun ideas, recipes, or activities you'd like to try — books, newspapers, lifestyle magazines, websites, and television shows offer near-constant ideas.

• *Hospitality: Clues for the Clueless* (Barbour) is a fun book that's filled with hospitality ideas. From parties to reaching out to your neighbors to celebrating everyday events, this book offers easy ideas you'll have fun putting into practice.

Chapter Seven: How You Connect — The Value of Community

• *Your Home a Lighthouse* by Bob and Betty Jacks (NavPress) is a thorough guide for hosting an evangelistic Bible study in your home. If you're looking for friends and want to reach out to unbelievers, starting a Bible study is a great way to do it.

• The book of Acts tells the story of how the early church was formed. Community — like the kind described in Acts 2:44-47 — was an integral part of the church's growth. Take some time to read Acts and talk together about what made the community of the early church so effective.

• *What's Your Story? An Interactive Guide to Building Authentic Relationships* (Piñon Press) is our first book and is filled with essays, journal pages, dialogues, and questions, all designed to get groups of people to tell their stories to one another and to build community.

229

CHAPTER EIGHT: WHAT YOU BELIEVE — SPIRITUALITY AND MARRIAGE

• *Feeding the Soul* by Jean Fleming (NavPress) is a fantastic handbook for quiet times. She explains why quiet time is so important to our walk with God and guides readers through developing good quiet-time practices. Reading this book will jump-start your time with God and give you renewed enthusiasm for this vital spiritual discipline.

• *Rocking the Roles: Building a Win-Win Marriage* by Robert Lewis and William Hendricks (NavPress) examines what the Bible says about male and female roles in marriage. It looks at common myths and misunderstandings about marriage roles, what submission is and isn't, and what's involved in spiritual leadership. The newly revised version includes discussion questions, making it ideal for using within a group.

• There are a lot of devotionals written for couples. The following are just a few we found at our local Christian bookstore. *Becoming Soul Mates: Cultivating Spiritual Intimacy in the Early Years of Marriage* by Les and Leslie Parrott (Zondervan) is a weekly devotional designed to help couples build a strong foundation for their marriage. *Quiet Times for Couples* by H. Norman Wright (Harvest House) has daily devotionals for a year. *Daily Marriage Builders for Couples* by Fred and Florence Littauer (Word) includes 120 devotional readings focused on marriage. *Moments Together for Couples* by Dennis and Barbara Rainey (Regal) is a daily devotional. Check your local bookstore for one that suits you best.

How to Use This Book with a Group or Another Couple

A lot of people will probably go through this book together as a couple, but if you want to go through it with a group of friends or even just one other couple, the following are a few ideas that should help make that a fun and productive experience.

- It might be a good idea to find a facilitator. Maybe that's you. A facilitator asks questions, keeps the discussion going, draws out people who may be shy about sharing, and is willing to go first when no one else wants to. A facilitator also helps plan important details like where you'll meet and who's bringing food.

- Find a few friends (or potential friends) to work through the book together. Maybe these are other engaged couples or couples who've recently married. Your enthusiasm will get everyone else excited about it too.

- Set a time (weekly, biweekly, monthly) to get everyone together. It works best to set a regular time to meet and get it scheduled in advance. Everyone is so busy that if you don't set up regular times to meet, it may be difficult or impossible to get everyone together.

• Set some ground rules for the group. Talk about things like purpose (why you're all getting together), participation (make sure everyone has a similar idea of what it means to be part of the group), attendance (how important it is for everyone to be there each time you meet), confidentiality (make sure that what's said in the group stays in the group), and accessibility (how open everyone is to being available to the other members of the group).

232 • Encourage group members to get together between regular meetings, send e-mails, or make occasional phone calls to each other. This will continue to build those friendships and will make your times together more fun and a little more comfortable for everyone.

• If you sense that someone isn't really into the group or is losing interest, take the time to ask him or her what's up. The reason for the disconnect may be something easy to fix.

• Different people in your group are going to have different communication styles and comfort levels when it comes to sharing their thoughts about the issues presented in this book. Be sensitive to these differences. You may have to do a little extra work to draw out a quiet person or to make sure the more vocal members of the group don't bury them.

After things get going, feel free to let others try their hand at facilitation. That will increase their ownership in the group and will give you a chance to sit back and participate without the responsibility for keeping things moving.

As a group, decide which chapter (or chapter subsections) you want to cover each time you get together. You may want to schedule your interactions with the book like this:

Week 1 — Read through the chapter text and discuss your thoughts on what you've read.

Week 2 — Answer the discussion questions as a group. Be willing to share tips from the chapter that worked well (or didn't work well) for you.

233

Week 3 — Read the "Voice of Wisdom" section for the chapter. Maybe ask an older couple to come to your group and give his or her perspective on the issue too.

You can repeat this pattern for each chapter of the book, but you can also take the book in smaller chunks or larger ones, depending on how many weeks you want to commit to getting together.

You may want to ask a few older couples to participate in your group to bring a different and experienced perspective to your discussions. Feel free to ask these older couples a lot of questions — they've been there and usually have great insight they're happy to share with younger couples.

Regardless of how you decide to structure your time together, keep in mind that when you're covering issues as interesting and personal as marriage, it may be difficult to get as much done as you'd hoped to during each meeting. If it takes you twice as long to get through a chapter as you thought it would, that's probably a good thing. It means everyone is really getting into it!

When we've participated in groups focused on marriage, we've found that couples often get stuck thinking there's a right and wrong way to approach some issues. But as we've listened to different perspectives and ways of doing things, we've learned a lot and found some helpful ideas that have added to our own marriage.

We hope you choose to use this book with a group and in the process make friends for a lifetime!

About the Authors

Toben and Joanne Heim were engaged the night before Joanne graduated from high school. They were married in 1991 and spent their honeymoon in Carmel, California, before returning to Whitworth College, their first apartment, and the task of writing a million (okay, not quite a million, but close!) thank-you notes.

The Heims graduated from Whitworth College in Spokane, Washington, where Toben majored in communication studies and Joanne majored in communication studies and French. While there, Toben served as the student body vice president and Joanne worked as the editor in chief of the college newspaper. Needless to say, their first year of marriage was a hectic one!

After graduating from college in 1993, they moved to Paris where Joanne worked as the software training coordinator for a French company, Le Bihan et Cie. They lived in a tiny studio apartment near Montparnasse, furnished with a desk, a hat rack, a television, and a mattress on the floor. Despite sparse living conditions, they had the best summer of their lives and spent rainy weekends wandering through the cemeteries and museums of Paris.

The Heims currently live in Southern California where Toben is the vice president of marketing at Youth Specialties, Inc., and Joanne is a full-time mother to their two daughters, Audrey and Emma.

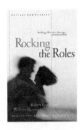